Dr. Webster-Doyle's

Martial Arts Guide for Parents

International Praise for Dr. Terrence Webster-Doyle's Work

Dr. Webster-Doyle has been awarded the Robert Burns Medal for Literature by Austria's Albert Schweitzer Society, for "outstanding merits in the field of peace promotion.

> "Dr. Webster-Doyle takes the reader beyond the physical aspects of Karate training to a discovery of self. His books are an asset to Martial Arts Instructors, students and parents of all styles, ages and rank levels."—Marilyn Fierro, 6th Dan; Owner and Chief Instructor, Smithtown Karate Academy, Smithtown, NY

Winner of Benjamin Frankin Awards for Excellence in Independent Publishing.

> "These topics are excellent and highly relevant. If each of the major countries of the world were to have ten Drs. Webster-Doyle, world peace is guaranteed to be achieved over a period of just one generation."—Dr. Chas. Mercieca, Executive Vice-President, International Ass'n of Educators for World Peace, NGO, United Nations (ECOSOC), UNICEF & UNESCO

Acclaimed at the Soviet Peace Fund Conference in Moscow and published in Russia by Moscow's Library of Foreign Literature and Magister Publications.

> "Every publication from the pen of this author should make a significant contribution to peace within and without. Highly recomended!"—*New Age Publishers and Retailers Alliance Trade Journal*

Why is Everybody Always Picking on Me? was cited by the Omega New Age Directory as one of the Ten Best Books of 1991 for its "atmosphere of universal benevolence and practical application."

Dr. Webster-Doyle's

Martial Arts Guide for Parents

Helping your Children Resolve Conflict Peacefully

---

by

Terrence Webster-Doyle

New York • Weatherhill • Tokyo

First edition, 1999

Published by Weatherhill, Inc., 41 Monroe Turnpike, Trumbull, CT 06611.

99 00 01 02 03 5 4 3 2 1

Library of Congress Cataloging-in-Publication Data available.

Contents

INTRODUCTION

We Want Our Children to Be Safe

As a response to young people being victimized by bullies, more and more parents are choosing to enroll their children in martial arts schools. But are these schools really teaching children what they need to understand and resolve conflict peacefully? We want our children to be safe. We want them to be self-confident and capable. We want them to acquire good values, to respect themselves and others, and to act with kindness and integrity in their relationships.

Can the study of martial arts teach them these things? Can the notoriously combative practice of martial arts skills create an environment of peace and well-being? Is it possible that such "arts" of aggression can give our children the skills to resolve conflict nonviolently? Can they enhance our children's ability to learn healthy and humane values?

The answer is yes, to each of these questions—but *only* if the martial arts are taught as a comprehensive system, a total program. Conventional methods being taught today are not living up to this potential. And because of this, they are doing more harm for your children than good in helping them to resolve conflict peacefully. Most martial arts schools today focus mainly on physical self-defense skills, with little or no information presented about how to deal with conflict *before* it becomes a physical confrontation. It is lopsided teaching, and our children suffer for it. This will be a main concern in this book—the martial arts *have* to be taught as a whole endeavor, both mentally and physically, if our children are to learn to resolve conflict without violence. For the most part, this is not being done.

Studying only physical self-defense skills is good for the body, but it ignores the preventive medicine we need for the mind.

Only when students receive instruction in how to prevent and resolve conflict combined with the study of physical self-defense skills do the martial arts become an excellent, and complete, educational tool for young people. Then they learn the skills to avoid being hurt physically *and* emotionally. The combination of physical and mental skills engages their bodies and minds while making them feel more confident, more self-assured, more focused. It is not a case of "either/or," but rather that both skills must be intelligently taught and developed.

As a parent, educator, author, and martial artist, I am determined that vitally needed mental skills be taught side-by-side with physical self-defense skills, to create a *whole* martial arts education. This is the way martial arts were originally taught when they were created centuries ago, and this is how they were meant to be learned. Presented in this way, the martial arts are capable of addressing one of most important social concerns in the world today—violence. It is true that the martial arts can also improve physical fitness and coordination and provide many other benefits. But its *main* intent is to teach people about conflict—what one can do to avoid, resolve, and manage it.

This Book Is Your Guide

I have written this book to help you understand what martial arts can offer when properly taught and therefore enable you to find the right martial arts program for your children. Some of you may be skeptical about the study of martial arts at all. Others may be concerned about the violence you have seen in martial arts movies and on television. I want to assure you that when these ancient arts are properly taught, they can teach your child to handle conflict not only now, but as an adult, years from now. My intention is to guide you in understanding why:

> *Conventional martial arts training does not help young people understand and resolve conflict peacefully. Young people need a complete conflict and values education to help them live healthier and happier lives.*

The purpose of this book is educate you about the peaceful potential of studying martial arts, and to help you become knowledgeable about what to expect when choosing a martial arts school for your children. As an involved parent, I know that you don't want to send them to a martial arts school without first knowing whether that school is teaching your children an "eye for an eye" approach to resolving conflict or teaching them to understand, resolve, and manage conflict intelligently and nonviolently.

CHAPTER 1

The Seriousness of Bullying

DEKALB, MISSOURI.

Twelve-year-old Nathan D. Faris pulled a gun from a duffel bag, fatally shot Timothy Perrin, 13, and took his own life by shooting himself. Faris had been the victim of relentless teasing by classmates.

EDINBORO, PENNSYLVANIA.

A month before shooting students at an eighth-grade dance, 14-year-old Andrew Wurst reportedly led friends to a dresser drawer, pulled out a gun, and told them he intended to kill people who had made him feel small.

JONESBORO, ARKANSAS.

Friends said that Mitchell Johnson, age 13, was angry about being rejected by a girl and warned a day before the tragedy that "he had a lot of killing to do." Johnson, whose parents were divorced, was known as a bully and a braggart, but he was also teased for being fat.

SPRINGFIELD, OREGON.

Kipland Phillip Kinkel, a 15-year-old who had been arrested for possession of a stolen firearm, walked into his school cafeteria, pulled a .22-caliber rifle from under a khaki trench coat and calmly fired more than 50 rounds among the 400 teenagers present. Two boys died and 23 other youngsters were injured. Later, a search of the Kinkel family home turned up the bodies of his parents, William Kinkel, 59, and Faith Kinkel, 57. News reports said Kinkel was angry at being teased by older students.

There had been signs of trouble. Kip Kinkel reportedly bragged about lighting a firecracker in a cat's mouth, killing the animal. A classmate said that when she returned from a vacation at Disneyland, Kip told her, "I want to kill Mickey Mouse." Jason Lott, a 15-year-old student, had gone hunting with Kip when they were both in seventh grade. "He'd say, 'I'm going to blow up your house.' He was pretty destructive, always blowing up stuff. My friend told me he blew up a dead cow—put a bomb in its stomach." Kip's middle school yearbook labeled him "Most Likely to Start World War III."

LITTLETOWN, COLORADO.

"There was blood everywhere." Eric Harris, age 18, and Dylan Klebold, age 17, two students at Columbine High School armed with guns and bombs, laid seige to their fellow students with a relentless fury for hours of terror, killing a teacher and 12 students while wounding 23 other students. Harris and Klebold casually decided which of their classmates should live and which should die, and laughed triumphantly as they dealt out their fate. They made at least two female hostages answer a question: did they belive in God? When the students answered yes, the gunmen excecuted them at point blank range. At the end of the terror both of the gunmen ended their own lives by shooting themselves. It took days to find the homemade bombs these teenage killers left at the school in order to create more carnage. This was the most lethal school shooting in history. The two young men who killed their fellow students with such an insane rage were outcasts who had been picked on, taunted, and harrassed by a certain segment of popular students.

Victims Who Became Bullies

The 1988 shooting in DeKalb, Missouri, was a singular and shocking event. The rest of the stories you've just read happened much more recently. Today, horrific reports like these are becoming more common, though no less shocking. The carnage in Springfield, Oregon, represented the sixth time in an eight-month period that one of America's public schools had been the scene of a fatal shooting. It wasn't even the only schoolyard killing *that week*. A few days before, a high school senior in Fayetteville, Tennessee, fatally wounded a student in the school parking lot.

One Springfield, Oregon, freshman had gone to the high school cafeteria, as usual, for a doughnut, milk, and gossip before classes started. When she stood to discard her empty milk container, she heard what sounded like firecrackers and turned to look straight into the eyes of a boy aiming a rifle just over her shoulder. She thought it was a prank at first. As bodies began falling around her, she just stood there, paralyzed.

Just a week earlier, her mother, frightened by the rash of school shootings in other parts of the country, had urged her daughter to be careful. The girl promptly dismissed the warning as pure melodrama. "Who in this town, in this school, would shoot at me?" she asked. The answer is Kipland Phillip Kinkel, a freckle-faced 15-year-old.

Then came the Columbine High School killings, so bizarre and so methodically planned over the course of a year, and then carried out with such Ramboesque precision that it riveted the whole country in collective horror. And, unfortunately, by the time this book appears, that nightmare may be superseded by even more terrible acts of violence in our halls of education.

Examining these many frightening stories more carefully, we can perceive common threads. Many of the reputed teenaged killers are reported to have felt like "outsiders." They were not star athletes or school leaders but kids who were out of the mainstream—unhappy, searching for their places in life, and suffering ridicule. Each felt like a "nobody" who desperately wanted to be a "somebody."

News reports said Kinkel was angry about being teased by older students. Another alleged killer was known as a bully and a braggart, but he was also teased for being fat. Luke Woodham, who allegedly killed two students and wounded seven in his Pearl, Mississippi, high school, was a chubby child who got picked on frequently. Michael Carneal, who is suspected of killing three students and wounding five others at West Paducah High School in Kentucky, was a fidgety, bespectacled young man sometimes described by peers as a "dweeb."

"I am not insane. I am angry," said a note from Luke Woodham. "I killed because people like me are mistreated every day."

The Availability of Firearms

These young people also have a far greater chance of getting their hands on deadly weapons than they did fifty years ago. The number of firearms in circulation nationwide has jumped from about 54 million in 1950 to an estimated 192 million today—far faster than the growth of the population.

Gun ownership was common in Springfield, Oregon. According to a phone poll in 1996, about 53% of all homes in Lane County had firearms, the same as the rest of Oregon. A close friend of Bill Kinkel said the father had recently bought Kip a rifle to teach him gun safety.

The apparent increase in high profile incidents over the past few years has prompted a variety of new approaches to reducing violence. A Department of Education study reported that 53% of public schools control access to school buildings and 4% now conduct random metal-detector searches on students. Discipline has been toughened too. In 1994, Congress enacted the Federal Gun-Free Schools Act, which encouraged states to pass laws mandating expulsion for students who bring guns to school. Massachusetts introduced a zero-tolerance weapons policy in late 1994, and the expulsion rate there jumped by over 50% in a year.

Although there is encouraging evidence that the approach has kept some guns out of schools, educators are naturally concerned that attention needs to be paid to students after they've been expelled. However, guns are a symptom; expelling young people when they bring a gun to school is not addressing the problem at its roots. My concern is helping young people understand and resolve conflict peacefully, to find acceptable, nondestructive ways to cope with anger *before* they are expelled, *before* they feel the need to find and use a gun.

The Inability to Express Anger

I have reviewed the horrifying incidents of Pearl, Mississippi; Paducah, Kentucky; Jonesboro, Arkansas; Springfield, Oregon, and Littleton, Colorado—places we would never expect to hear about such crimes—in an to attempt to understand these children and their motivation. In all cases, they are examples of young people who commit murder because they are not able to express anger and frustration in more socially responsible ways. They have not had a proper education in understanding themselves, in coping with conflict and bullying peacefully. We teach them the "3Rs, " but we neglect the "4th R" — relationships.

The common factor linking all these young people is that they were victims of bullying—and then they became bullies, with guns.

Schools are experiencing a proliferation of violence. Could it be that bullying, often disregarded by both parents and teachers as a serious problem, is a strong contributing factor? Bullying by children and violence by teens are on the rise. Between 1979 and 1989, there was a 61% increase in shooting deaths committed by U.S. youths aged 15 to 19. A survey conducted in 1994, of 204 middle and high school students in several Midwestern communities, indicated that 75% of those surveyed said they had been bullied.

Bullying not only affects children while they are young but also sets a pattern for adult life. Studies show that bullies, if not stopped, are far more likely than non-bullies to grow up to be violent, abusive adults. Gang-related violence is an early form of bullying that ultimately can lead to family, community, and even global conflict.

Defeating the Bully

The story following relates how I discovered my own strength. Although I am nearly sixty years old, the events remain vivid in my mind, and every time I recall them, I realize that my ability to defeat bullies was discoverd on that day. I call the story "Saved by the Bee."

"Saved by the Bee"

An Incident that Changed my Life Forever

I remember, like it was yesterday, the day that changed my life forever. I was running, and I knew he was right behind me and would catch me. I felt like an animal being hunted. I couldn't run faster. I was scared and out of breath. He had one thing in mind — to get me — again! I felt humiliated and ashamed of myself as I ran.

I felt Vinnie's heavy breath on my back. He caught me from behind, pulling me backward to the hard ground. My instincts were to try to protect myself from being hurt, and not to fight back. Fighting back would only make him angry. Then he might really hurt me, as his brother did when he knocked out my front teeth with a rock the year before, and the time before that when Vinnie purposely ran into me with his bike. I ended up in the hospital with a severe head injury that has caused me problems to this day.

He pinned me down with his knees on my chest. Sitting on top of me, he began punching my face. I tried to cover my face with my hands; that's all I could do. I felt so helpless! All of a sudden, I felt a sharp pain in my back as if I had fallen on a hot needle.

I jumped up without thinking, yelling in agony. A bee had stung me! I stood there for a moment in shock, trying to reach the wounded area with my hand. Then I remembered what was happening just moments before the sting. I felt an overwhelming sense of fear. But it ended suddenly when I realized that Vinnie, the bully who had plagued me throughout elementary school, wasn't beating me up. In fact, he lay stunned on his back where I had thrown him when I jumped up after being stung.

I looked down at him and felt a sudden surge of power. I realized at that moment that I was strong. I understood that I had let this person beat me up because I *thought* I was weak. In my mind I had seen myself as a victim. It was an awe-inspiring feeling, and it changed my life.

Vinnie must have read that feeling in my face, for his eyes were now wide with fear. He moved away, crawling backward. He then got up and, still facing me, moved cautiously down the street. Without a word, he left me standing alone in the yard where only minutes ago he had been beating me up. He still called me names, but only from afar, and he never came close to me again.

I think about what I could have done to stop being bullied. I didn't want to fight and I wasn't a fast runner. Believing I had no other choice, I let myself be beat up. Looking back on it now, I think that I could have used my brain to prevent myself from being bullied. Since then, I've learned nonviolent alternatives, and I've had the opportunity to roleplay many conflict situations that have taught me how to help young people prevent such incidents. Today, I think that I really could have stood up to those bullies, but back then, I had no idea how.

It's hard to know what would have worked. But anything my imagination could have thought up would have been better than all the beatings I got. It took a great deal of time to work through those feelings.

Victims of bullying rarely fight back. However, a bullied victim suffers physically and emotionally and is so full of rage that he or she, down the road, can become a bully, too.

A child who is continually bullied not only suffers physical bruises and mental anguish but often becomes a bully too, to "get back" or "release the anger" that has built up from being treated so brutally. That was certainly the case with me, and that is why I want to help you prevent this from happening to your children.

All I Was Taught to Do

When I was growing up outside New York City in the 40s and 50s, there were no martial arts schools where I could have learned how to protect myself. But what if there had been? What if I had been taught physical self-defense, which is what most martial arts teach today? How would my struggles with Vinnie have turned out?

I can imagine it now. I see the bully coming, looking to beat me up. Do I assume the victim's mentality of always losing? Do I feel trapped? Probably. But the confidence I gained by learning physical self-defense might have allowed me to keep my cool and not be quite so overwhelmed by my natural instinct to survive. I probably would have stood my ground, gone into a martial arts fighting stance in preparation for combat and defended myself.

But what would this have accomplished? Would I have been able to protect myself from getting beaten up? Or would the bully have been too tough or skilled a fighter to beat? In New York, many street fighters were very good at what they did. Still, solid martial arts physical defense skills can be very effective—so much that they might really hurt a bully. A well placed kick to the groin, a palm heel to the chin, or a strike to the temple area might be very damaging, even lethal. But the bully asked for it, didn't he? And that would be all I could do, because that would have been all I was taught to do.

Perhaps my martial arts school might have taught me enough physical self-defense skills to make me feel confident enough to walk away from a fight. Looking back, I don't think so. With Vinnie, there wasn't a chance to walk away. There was no other alternative but to fight. But I continue to imagine what I might have done to avoid that situation.

- *Is there anything I could have done before the beating happened?*
- *If I could not avoid a confrontation, could I have resolved it using verbal skills?*
- *Was my only alternative to fight?*
- *Once it started, could I have managed it better?*

Forty Years Later, the Answer

With the escalating violence young people face today, I believe that resolving conflict *without* fighting is the best way, simply because it is the safest way. There are people who believe that if a child is taught physical self-defense skills, that child has the ability to resolve conflict without fighting. I cannot agree. My forty years of experience have taught me an important truth:

We cannot stop conflict with physical abilities alone.

We need to learn the mental martial arts. In addition to learning blocks, kicks, and punches, we have to learn skills that will help us resolve conflict peacefully *before* it gets to the physical level.

This requires that we use the most powerful weapon we own—our brains.

Our children can learn practical skills that help them develop the presence of mind to *understand* and *avoid* conflict. They have the ability to develop and use verbal skills as a means of self-protection. These skills engage their minds and make them feel powerful. It's as simple as that.

I only wish that I could have studied the martial arts, a complete program, when I was young—not to beat up Vinnie and his brother, but to feel the power of knowing how to prevent a fight from happening. It's too late for that, But what I *can* do is help your children make this discovery before it's too late for them. I hope you will pass the information in this book on to them so that they have a better chance than I did of growing up confident, healthy, and happy.

CHAPTER 2

Why Conventional Martial Arts Programs Don't Work

Let's say that your children want to learn the martial arts. You look in the *Yellow Pages*, under "martial arts," and see a confusing number of ads promising many spectacular things:

BECOME A BLACK BELT!
TOTAL SELF DEFENSE!
TURN FEAR INTO POWER!
CARDIO KICKBOXING!
UNSEAL YOUR POTENTIAL!
THE PATH OF TRANSFORMATION!
UNLEASH YOUR HIDDEN DESIRES!
GRAND MASTER INSTRUCTORS!
ONE-HIT TOUCH KNOCKOUTS!
TOO DANGEROUS FOR TOURNAMENTS!

Your brain reels from the choices. So, you decide to visit some schools personally.

The "Grand Master" School in the Mall

The martial arts school you visit is probably in a mall. There are several grandiose trophies in the window. You see a sign that promises "A BLACK BELT IN ONLY TWO YEARS!" — but only if you join a special club.

Upon entering you are greeted by a muscled young man, perhaps in his mid-twenties. In a military manner, he begins to bark out the reasons one should study martial arts. He is dressed in a bright red satin outfit with gold trim and, around his waist, he wears a large black belt whose ends hang down to his knees. Written on the belt is his name in gold lettering.

You try to explain to him that you are seeking a school for your children and not yourself, but his high-pressured sales pitch doesn't let you off the hook. He shows you around the posh athletic club. There is an array of body-building equipment around the room. Mirrors cover most of the walls. On the other walls there are large photos of well known action film stars shaking hands with the young man who is giving you the tour. The inscriptions read "To Grand Master Smith" and are signed by the movie star. You realize that this young man in his twenties is already a "Grand Master."

He invites you into his office to tell you about the children's class.

The High-Pressured Sales Pitch

"Your children will get the best training possible to prepare them for success in life. Our goal is to empower them to learn, to lead, to win," he says. His tone of voice becomes almost zealous, as if practicing the martial arts were a patriotic duty. He then pulls out a contract.

"Mrs. Jones, you don't want your children to be failures, do you? You want to empower them to be successful, don't you? There are many dangerous people out there waiting to take advantage of your children. You want your children to turn their fear into power, don't you, Mrs. Jones? Our martial arts system is the best in the world! Ours is the original!

"My Great Grand Master's Great Grand Master began this style for the Emperor of Siam. Its royal lineage has been handed down to me. I am the last descendent of the line of Great Grand Masters. Your children will study with the best. I will prepare them for the real world. Allow your children to study martial arts with me and they will have success in all of life—whether in the board room, the classroom, or the street. Their spiritual life will also be enhanced!"

You listen to the barrage of claims and feel even more overwhelmed. You are told that if you sign a multiyear contract right now, you are elegible for the Golden Eagle Plan, through which you and your entire family can enter his specially reserved Black Belt Honor Society that guarantees you all black belts in only two years or less.

The Military Approach

Sensing that you are unsure of what to do and unwilling to sign a contract, he invites you to stay for the two children's classes about to begin—simultaneously. One is called Tiny Golden Dragons, for ages three to five. The other, for ages six to ten, is called Ninja Warriors. He invites you to sit in a one-way, glass-enclosed waiting room that overlooks the carpeted area.

You have a moment to look around as he excuses himself for a moment and talks to an even younger man, perhaps in his mid-teens, who also wears a satin outfit with a large black belt.

You then notice, attached to the black belt of the Grand Master, a cellular phone which he uses constantly while talking to the other young man.

Young children and their parents start to enter the room as if on signal. The children are dressed in black outfits wearing different colored belts. They all have many stripes on their belts and many patches of their uniforms. On the back of their uniforms is written the name of the school in large, bright red letters, making each child a walking advertisement. Some of the older students, ages eight to ten, have long, narrow black bags which, you discover, contain martial arts weapons: spears, short swords, wooden sticks attached with chains, long swords, and an array of weapons you have never seen before. You then notice that at the end of the room there is a display of numerous deadly weapons.

The parents sit dutifully at the end of the carpeted area while the children quickly line up upon a command from the younger instructor. The Grand Master is busy on his cell phone. The young man barks out a military-like order in a foreign language, and the children suddenly come to attention. Patriotic, soldierly music blasts from the loud speakers placed around the room. Then everyone salutes a photo that hangs between two flags. The photo is of an ancient-looking man in a red satin outfit. Then they bow and all repeat after the young instructor some programmed slogan in the foreign language.

The music stops. Then there is silence for a minute after which the children sit and close their eyes in a meditative way while the young man guides them in a short praise of the founder of this martial art. Suddenly the music begins again from the speakers but this time it is rock and roll. The young man barks a command, and the children jump to their feet in a combat position, yelling loudly in unison as they do. He then moves from group to group, giving commands to each.

The younger group, the Tiny Golden Dragons, practices acrobatic moves, their tiny bodies trying hard to do kicks and punches that seem too difficult for them. When the Ninja Warriors are instructed to practice using their weapons, they get them out and twirl them about in fancy movements. You notice that there is barely enough room for the students because there are so many of them. The whirling blades, sticks, chains, and knives come precariously close to the students as they work to perform to the rhythm of the blaring music.

You sit there half-mesmerized by the dazzling effects of this martial arts display and wonder if you should check out other schools, just for comparison's sake, since you don't feel you know much about the martial arts in the first place. You are impressed with the acrobatic gymnastics of these young children and their zealous dedication. But in your heart, you wonder if this martial arts school is sending the proper message.

You stay the whole forty-five minutes of the class, after which another group of kids rushes in to begin another cycle of exactly what you witnessed in the first class. You notice that the head teacher is paying no attention to the classes. You slip out, fortunately unnoticed by the young Grand Master, who is deeply engrossed in his telephone conversation, and you take a deep breath of air once you are outside the crowded mall.

Why You Must Do Your Own Checking

I have visited hundreds of martial arts schools around the world over the years, and I have seen many that resemble this school. Yet there are many fine schools and instructors trying to do good things for their students. But unfortunately there are too many like the one just described, and most people looking for a martial arts school do not have the experience to tell the good from the bad. And some are really bad. Some martial arts schools are cult-like endeavors that condition young people to worship exalted "Grand Masters" simply because they come from an exotic, foreign place.

A very famous cult leader recently held a conference for Martial Artists in the United States that cost more than a million dollars. His organization invited hundreds of recognized Martial Artists from all over the world to participate in this conference, and used it to announce that he was going to "take over" the martial arts.

I suspect he knows that every day hundreds of thousands of children are being conditioned in quasi-military environments by uneducated, money-driven martial arts instructors to give their obedience to ways of living that are undemocratic. He knows that these children are one step away from potentially embracing his cult philosophy. Thousands already have made this man very rich. I think he knows that these conditioned young people could be his next generation of cult followers.

There are all sorts of unethical martial arts business schemes to get your money and to keep you and your children taking classes. They practice intimidation, promise excessive rewards and utilize high-pressure tactics. Martial arts teaching in the United States, and throughout most of the world for that matter, is completely unregulated. In other words, anyone can go out today, without any martial arts experience at all, buy a martial arts outfit and a black belt, open a school, and begin teaching children. There is no authority assessing or certifying their capability or qualifications for this important work.

Do you know the so-called "masters" teaching your children?

Do you know what your children are being taught?

In order to teach in a public school, one needs a proper college education—a degree and knowledge of how to teach, certified by the state. Also often required is an FBI checkup to see whether a potential teacher has ever committed a crime.

In a martial arts school, instructors need no real education; they are not required to know anything about the development of young children. There is nobody checking how teachers teach, how or if they use proper lesson plans, or whether they carry any legitimate certification. No one receives a criminal background check.

The teaching of martial arts is not regulated, but it should be, not by politicians, but by a coalition of educators, counselors, law enforcement officers, school administrators, parents, and martial arts teachers. In this way, working for the good of our youth and the community, these regional "coalitions" could help martial arts teachers obtain the proper education and certification to be valid martial arts educators.

Martial arts instructors need to understand, both for themselves and for their students, how to resolve conflict peacefully —the true intent of all martial arts.

What Should Martial Arts Schools Teach?

Perhaps you have been concerned how much your children are exposed to graphic violence on TV and in the movies—violence that goes far beyond what you experienced as a young person.

Maybe you believe that, somewhere along the way, the producers of these movies and television shows crossed over the line of decency. You have been long aware that while the moral education of young people is given less emphasis, some musicians even *advocate* outright violence in music that is sold to the young and very impressionable buyer.

Now, your child wants to study martial arts, and you are concerned. You want a martial arts school for your child that will:

- *Teach physical skills that will give your child a sense of confidence.*
- *Teach your child how to intelligently cope with bullying at school.*
- *Teach positive social values: respect, honesty, humility, and dignity.*
- *Help your child to get along with others and to treat others with respect.*
- *Familarize your child with the "old-fashioned" ethics you learned when you grew up.*

The Importance of Asking Questions

At a martial arts school, children need to be taught the importance of learning things on their own. They should be encouraged to take the time to ask questions so that they can discover answers for themselves. As you search for an appropriate school for your child, I suggest that you do this as well.

Below is a sampling of the types of questions you will want to ask at any school you visit. If you don't get satisfactory answers, continue your search until you find the right place for your child. Take the time to visit as many martial arts schools in your areas as you can. There are many capable, well educated martial arts teachers. More and more martial arts instructors are realizing the need to teach young people complete conflict education skills. They are recognizing that these skills are necessary to help their students cope with bullying and violence in their relationships.

My hope is that we parents, by educating *ourselves* about what is proper martial arts training for our children, will search out the right teachers for them. In so doing, we will advance the evolution of the martial arts to meet the current challenges our children face every day.

Finally, when you look for martial arts schools in the *Yellow Pages,* move away from the spectacular ads promising the outlandish and the incredible. Look for ads that promise something better, like "Martial arts for Peace. Teach your children how to understand and resolve conflict peacefully." Visit those schools, and don't forget your list of questions.

Questions for Candidates for Martial Arts Instructor of your Child

1. What are your basic goals in teaching children the martial arts?
2. How, specifically, do you accomplish these goals?
3. How do you teach young people to understand and resolve conflict *before* it becomes a physical confrontation?

4. What specific skills do you teach children to avoid conflict?

5. What specific skills do you teach them to resolve conflict?

6. Do you teach only physical skills? If so, do you believe these can help young people prevent conflict from happening? How?

7. If my child learns only physical self-defense skills, will he or she have the confidence to walk away from a potential fight? What happens if a bully follows my child?

8. Do you think that educating the mind of your students is just as important as training their bodies?

9. If yes, then how do you go about educating their minds, specifically?

10. What does a child have to do for rank advancement? Do you evaluate a student on his or her ability to learn mental skills as well as physical ones?

11. May I sit in and observe a class or two?

12. What are your financial requirements? Are there any special arrangements? Any additional fees down the road?

13. What is your contractual arrangement? How long must we sign up for? Do the fees escalate at some point?

14. If we have to move in six months, is the contract easily terminated? What if my child gets sick, or for whatever reason is unable to continue taking classes? Are there penalties? Do you sell your contracts to a collection agency that will come after me if we cannot continue in the program?

CHAPTER 3

What "Martial Arts for Peace" Can teach Your Child

Let's now pay a visit to a school whose focus is on "Martial Arts for Peace." You arrive at a building in a pleasant neighborhood. You enter the school and notice a quietness, a gentle ambiance about it. The area inside has an office to one side, and a long empty room with a polished wooden floor. Paintings on the wall depict scenes from nature, while in the waiting area there is a display of books, curricula, magazines, and other educational materials.

On another wall are colorful posters. One of them shows a child being picked on by another child. Around this illustration is a series of phrases, such as: "Use Humor," "Reason with the Bully," "Make Friends," and "Walk Away with Confidence." Another poster shows children bowing to an older man. Surrounding this are sayings such as: "Respect is honoring the dignity of all life," "Kindness is caring for others as you would like to be cared for," and "Humility is acting without self-importance."

You are greeted by a man, perhaps in his fifties or early sixties. He appears to be in good shape. He is dressed in a clean, plain, white martial arts uniform, devoid of any patches except one over his heart reading "Martial Arts for Peace" around a sprig of green bamboo. Around his waist is a frayed black belt.

His manner is gentle and reassuring. He calls himself Dr. Johnson and asks what you've learned about the martial arts. He listens attentively to your explanation of the needs of your children. He asks if you have a moment to hear what he has to say.

He explains that although the martial arts have a "martial" history, they were originally arts of peace and self-understanding. They were practiced to help people resolve conflict without the use of violence. The way he teaches children is to give them a *whole* education in understanding and resolving conflict. He claims that physical skills should be taught to give a child the confidence to *not* fight. At this school, children are taught to use nonviolent alternatives.

He then outlines for you his total Conflict Education Program, which he refers to by the acronym **ARM.**

AVOIDING CONFLICT

Young people are first taught to understand conflict.
If they understand it, they can often avoid it.

RESOLVING CONFLICT

They next learn how to resolve conflict,
using their heads instead of their fists.

MANAGING CONFLICT

Lastly, they are taught to protect themselves,
if need be, through by the humane application
of self-defense skills.

He tells you that these first two levels of the total Conflict Education Program are complex skills that take at least as much time to learn as physical self-defense skills. He further explains that a complete conflict-education program develops in young people an ability to resolve conflict when they become adults.

Your host then shows you books and lesson plans that he and his instructors use. You are impressed with their quality. You notice particularly that there are no violent physical combat skills depicted in them, and you become aware that there are no violent martial arts magazines lying around.

When he asks whether you have any questions, you tell him your concerns about bullying and the lack of values you see today. He shows you his "Defeat the Bully the Smart Way" program, which teaches young people how to cope with being bullied. It has a section on manners and a chapter about the benefits of respectful behavior, called "Respect: The Act That Conquers Fear."

He tells you that a Martial Arts for Peace school emphasizes understanding and resolving conflict without the unnecessary use of physical force, that the intent of Martial Arts for Peace is to assist students in learning about the "martial" within themselves. In Martial Arts for Peace programs the focus is on understanding what *prevents* peace, that is, the conditioning that creates conflict—what it is, how it works, and what sustains it.

He then welcomes you to view an upcoming class. You are invited to sit in an open area in front of the wooden floor. You thumb through some of the books and see how they are arranged into stories explaining the peaceful philosophy of the martial arts. Some of the books are practical explanations of how to resolve conflict without the use of physical techniques. You notice in the back of one of the books that Dr. Johnson is a parent and a former school teacher. It also mentions that Dr. Johnson has been active in organizations working with and helping young people and that he has been practicing and teaching martial arts for many years.

You also notice that the books have received accolades and endorsements by prestigious organizations. The lesson plans for the teachers impress you and you can see that they are well laid out for those who teach and learn from them.

Signs of Respect

After a short while a group of young people, ages eight to twelve, come in, some with their parents and others with their friends. They are in their street clothes and carry bags along with their school books. The children take off their shoes and socks and, with great attention, place them on wooden shelves made for holding footwear. Then the children go to the separate boys' and girls' dressing rooms in the back of the larger room. They walk along the carpeted side that runs down one side of the room to the back. They do not walk on the wooden floor.

When the young people are dressed, they file out in an orderly way and bow before entering the wooden area. They go to a file where they take out a card and read it. Dr. Johnson explains that this card is their practice progression chart which allows them to monitor their advancement in the time before class. Dr. Johnson explains that he and the other instructors also monitor them by giving tests at certain times throughout the year. Rank advancement is based on how a child has progressed both mentally and physically. Insights and mental skills are an integrated part of the overall curriculum of the school.

Soon two other adults enter and politely introduce themselves to you. They are Dr. Johnson's assistant instructors. They appear to be in their mid-thirties. They too change into white uniforms that bear the same bamboo patch, and each wears a plain black belt.

The class comes to order when one of the teachers, a woman

with black hair, asks them to line up. The class lines up in order of rank, with the teachers sitting in front, facing the students. Everyone is quiet for a minute or two; then they all bow to each other respectfully.

The Gentle Art of Conflict Resolution

One of the assistant instructors leads the class in warm-ups and light stretching. Dr. Johnson and the other assistant move around the children demonstrating the proper way to warm up and stretch. After about fifteen minutes, they all begin to practice graceful, dancelike movements. There is no music, no saluting Grand Masters, no military commands. Instead there is gentle yet firm encouragement from each instructor. You are impressed by how equally and maturely the young people are treated. There seems to be no special reverence given to anyone, but mutual respect for everyone is obvious.

After about half an hour of physical work, the young people are asked to sit down in a semicircle. Dr. Johnson opens one of his books and reads a story. He then asks the students what they learned from it. They participate in an active dialogue that seems to engage them all. Dr. Johnson tells them that it is very important to educate the mind was well as the body, that the two go together.

Then, with the help of his assistants, he divides the students into two groups. They practice roleplaying the bully and the victim, and resolving conflict using verbal skills. They also learn to be aware of body language, how to recognize a potential foe, and to be aware of subtle danger signals that untrained people rarely notice.

Class ends with the practice of "forms," artistic physical movements that don't look martial at all. At the conclusion of class, everyone lines up to stretch again and to warm down. They sit quietly for a moment and then bow. The students calmly change into their street clothes and carefully take their shoes from the shoe rack. They individually bow to their teachers and leave.

After class Dr. Johnson thanks you for staying and invites you to attend again if you like. No contracts are shoved into your face, and no high pressure sales tactics are used. You are given a simple brochure to take with you about the school, classes, times and monthly fees. He also gives you a sheet titled: "Martial Arts for Peace: What We Do. What We Don't Do," which reads:

What We Do	What We Don't Do
Promote peaceful resolution of conflict.	Promote violent and aggressive behavior.
Learn to control ourselves through understanding.	Learn to control others through fear.
Teach nonviolent alternatives.	Teach how to maim and kill.
Solve conflict by using the brain.	Solve conflict by fighting.
Believe that cooperation is beneficial.	Believe that might is right.
Respect people of peace.	Emulate tough action heroes.

Question the value of playing at war to bring about peace.	Play with warlike toys or real martial arts weapons.
Promote healthy competition to challenge young people to be strong and confident.	Promote martial arts tournaments that are egoistic displays of warlike behavior.
Encourage young people to choose a martial arts school intelligently by inquiring into its programs.	Use superficial gimmicks and rewards to manipulate young people into taking martial arts classes.
Reward young people for the patience and effort it takes to learn a complex discipline.	Use behavioral-conditioning techniques (e.g., rank advancement) to keep students attending.
Teach children to develop healthy limits of aggression within a safe, trusting environment by practicing their martial arts techniques just short of full contact.	Teach children to go beyond their normal limits of aggression in a quasi-military environment and through full-contact fighting.
Teach young people healthy values of humility and integrity, and that respect comes from kindness and consideration.	Teach young people that to be a winner means being tough, aggressive, and in control, and that respect comes through having power and ambition.

CHAPTER 4

How to Alter the Conditioning that Causes Conflict

Let's explore this model of the Martial Arts for Peace school to see if its approach can provide what you wish for your children—that they acquire tools to ensure their personal safety along with sound values. The first thing we need to look at, to understand what *threatens* their personal safety, is conditioning— for it is the basic cause of conflict, of violence. What do we mean by conditioning? How does it come about, what sustains it, and what can Martial Arts for Peace do about it?

Whenever I go into schools to talk with children, I find that many have been culturally conditioned to admire the heroic ideal of fighting as a solution to conflict. This is hardly surprising, of course, since combat has traditionally been portrayed as the acceptable, indeed honorable, solution to the problems of relationships between good guys and bad guys. All media have exploited and glorified this interpretation in both factual and fictional presentations, as seen in cowboy movies and kung-fu flicks, detective dramas and cop shows, stories of war and adventure, and even on the evening news.

The Martial Arts for Peace Difference

At the Martial Arts for Peace school, it is understood that:

- *The martial arts are excellent vehicles for physical fitness. They are also fun and exciting sports, which do not have to be overly competitive.*

- *By developing one's ability to neutralize hostility through alternative, nonviolent means, mental self-defense skills provide a way to ethically and effectively respond to aggression.*

- *As a by-product of this unique type of physical and mental activity, the overall learning process is greatly enhanced; children taking our classes have shown a greater aptitude for scholastic endeavors.*

- *Children study self-defense skills to develop the confidence* not *to fight. Using roleplaying techniques, they are taught non-threatening ways to avoid conflict.*

The study of Martial Arts for Peace is an effective, nonviolent discipline. I am determined that our children learn it so that they become even more effective in dealing with conflict in their lives. The world in which we live can be a hostile place, and we want them to be able to deal with it from a position of strength.

The Ongoing Battle of Life

Children experience a great deal of violence through movies, TV, and video games. Because of this exposure to violent images, they often have nightmares that frighten them. Afterward, many are drawn again to war comics, violent video games, and scary movies. The attraction seems to result from a need to protect themselves from the frightening images of their dreams by becoming familiar with them, through reading more about them or watching them on screen.

At home, perhaps your family watches the news as it highlights the conflicts and violence in our world. The media present the world as a threatening and violent place, in which peril seeming lurks in every dark alley, every unlit parking lot, and every neighborhood at night, where "every stranger is a danger!" If you and your spouse work, perhaps you talk about how badly people treat one another on the job, at the supermarket, or on the street. Likely there is even, occasionally, obvious conflict between you two, or between you and your friends or neighbors.

On a daily basis, your children pledge their allegiance to their country, and told it must be defended against its enemies. Those who are good athletes are victorious in games and sports, and admired and befriended by classmates, while those who lack skills are ignored or teased. In the schoolyard, some children bully others; there's at least one fight every day.

This is a lot of aggression for young people to experience. Life feels like an ongoing battle. And in addition to these external struggles, we experience inner conflicts—the ones that gnaw at us from within, between the person we are taught we should be and the person we believe we really are. We flare up sometimes in anger and frustration without understanding why.

If *we* are having trouble understanding the reasons for our distress, imagine how difficult it is for our children, who lack our experience in life.

What is Conditioning?

We often feel torn apart, divided within ourselves and separated from each other. The reason for these feelings is our conditioning. It is the cause of conflict both within and of outside us, in our homes, in our communities, and throughout the world. It is a major factor in preventing us from fully enjoying the fruits of our democratic system, for democracy depends on the intelligent understanding of ourselves and others. A democracy presumes the right to question, to inquire freely, whereas our conditioning programs into us a rigid state of mind that hinders freedom of inquiry. In order to understand how our conditioning propels us inevitably toward those great conflicts called war, we must first learn to understand how conditioning creates the conflicts within us, and how it effects our relationships with others.

All conflict has its roots in this thing called "conditioning." To condition means to teach or to train. We have all been conditioned to stop when a traffic light turns red. Have you ever thought about how many times we, as children, had to be told to stop for a red light or to look before crossing the street before we were actually conditioned to remember it for ourselves? How many times in turn have you reminded your child to heed a red light, or look both ways before crossing a street?

Most of the thoughts in our mind and the actions we take every day are based on how we have been conditioned. We are conditioned to brush our teeth in the morning, to lock the door on our way out, to dress a certain way, and to greet each other in a certain manner.

We are all creatures of habit, with ingrained patterns of walking, talking, thinking, and acting.

There are three principal ways in which we are all conditioned and, therefore, three different kinds of conditioning:

Biological Conditioning. If we go too long without eating or drinking, we become hungry and weak, and will eventually die. Our body is naturally driven to get the food and water it needs to keep us alive. Our biological instinct is to survive, at all cost. This conditioning is involuntary. We are born with it; it is part of our nature. The fight-or-flight instinct, which helps protect us from danger, is also part of our biological conditioning.

Physiological Conditioning. In the course of our daily activities, we keep our bodies in shape by stretching, bending, reaching, jumping, running—by being active. We perform these activities automatically and almost effortlessly. If we engage in sports or other special activities, we condition our bodies to efficiently perform the movements required without thinking about them. As our bodies grow more accustomed to these activities, our muscles become "conditioned" to them. Thus we can modify the body's physiological (physical) capabilities.

Psychological Conditioning. We stop for a red light or brush our teeth before going to bed because we have been taught to do so. Behavior that is repeated becomes a habit. Something we may at one time have had to think about, we now do without thinking at all. Psychological conditioning is training of the mind, and may even employ a system of punishments and rewards to make us act in a habitual, predetermined way. Although we have perhaps heard of "Pavlov's dog" or incidents of "brainwashing" in totalitarian countries, most of us never stop to consider whether we can alter our mental conditioning. We can, and martial artists do.

Our Conditioning Creates Our Conflict

If a car moves rapidly toward us, we move out of its path as fast as we can; this is our biological conditioning at work. We are born with this brand of conditioning. It exists without our having to think about it, and there is not much we can do to change it. In this case, it is an automatic reaction that can save our life and is, therefore, positive.

Exercise tones the body and, undertaken on a regular basis, makes us feel good. Those who exercise, however, know that in the process of conditioning the body to perform positively, there can be negative effects. We may strain a muscle or tear a ligament. So, not all physiological conditioning is positive.

Psychological training is often very good. We teach our children to floss their teeth, to watch for oncoming vehicles when they cross the street, to say no to any stranger who offers them a ride. The mental training we received from our family, and the training we now give to our own children, is meant to be positive, for our own good and the good of our children. Sometimes, however, and perhaps without our knowing it, the things we have been taught, and the things we in turn teach, can have negative consequences.

For example, if you believe your child should "turn the other cheek" when threatened by a bully, I understand your nonviolent intentions. But if your child believes that fighting the bully is the way to deal with the situation, your child is in conflict. And this conflict may be causing your child great pain.

We, and our children, are mentally conditioned by what we see and what we are told. This conditioning determines how we think and feel, and how we think and feel determines how we act.

While accepting and understanding the way biological conditioning works, however, we don't have to be controlled by it. Just as we have control over our physical and mental conditioning, with the practice of the martial arts, we can have control over our biological impulses.

If we want to change our conditioning, all it takes is an interest in doing so, and understanding that such change is possible.

Conflict Is a Symptom of Fear

Perhaps you have an interest in changing something about the way your mind or the mind of your child has been conditioned; you understand that it can be changed, but you find the possibility a bit frightening. Fear can stop us in our tracks.

Fear is that strong feeling we get when we become aware of danger. Because the world in which we live can be violent, all of us have felt afraid of something or someone, or perhaps many things. Rest assured that all humans feel fear, even bullies. Fear is a fascinating part of our biological conditioning, and the cause of a lot of our conflict. It appears without our having any say about it, and once it appears, it creates reactions that can cause us to lose confidence. But fear is also an outcome of conditioned thinking, fearful ideas and images that have been programmed into us that can create conflict. These fearful and violent images can unnecessarily stimulate our biologically conditioned defense system, the fight-or-flight mechanism, because the images are taken as a real threat when in actuality they are not. When the threat is only a perceived one, not an actual one, when what we *think* rather than what actually *is* triggers our biological self-protective system, we get into trouble.

This is important to be aware of, for being stimulated to protect ourselves physically from a purely psychological "threat" has throughout history led human beings into wars. Essentially all wars have their roots in the division and opposition between established belief systems. We have been conditioned to envision followers of the other system as "the enemy," posing a threat real enough to justify our defending against it by killing. Just how we are conditioned to think and how our thinking triggers our biological self-defense system to protect us is important in understanding what *prevents* peace, and should be a central issue in all martial arts teachings.

The Fight-or-Flight Reaction

We have all watched a dog and cat when they first meet. They freeze. Then the cat either hisses and claws at the dog or runs away. The cat either fights or takes flight. We humans do the same thing. When we see we are facing an actual threat, we react in a fight-or-flight manner. In other words, our response to the threat is either to defend ourselves or to run away. This fight-or-flight mechanism is located deep in the layers of our brain, our primitive brain, the brain that has been passed down to us, generation through generation, since the beginning of mankind.

This fight-or-flight mechanism has a positive, very useful function. It protects us from injury by sending messages to those parts of the brain responsible for handling self-protective actions. In the days of our remote ancestors, the messages from the brain were either "There's a lion. Raise your spear!" or "The lion's charging. Run away!" Today, the messages from the brain are more often like, "That car better stop. I've got the green light!" or "Whoops, he's not stopping. Better get out of the way!" When a real physical threat come about, a powerful hormone, adrenaline, is secreted, which gives the body a quick burst of energy to carry out its survival tactics. So, the fight-or-flight response is a healthy function that can protect the body from harm.

The problem with this response, however, is that it is a function of our "old" brain, the part that has been passed down to us from our ancient human ancestors. The old brain's fight-or-flight response does not differentiate between a physical threat and a mental threat, that is, between an actual threat and a perceived threat—it just reacts. So, when we or our children see horrifying scenes on television or in film, scenes that frighten us, our fight-or-flight mechanism triggers a psychologically self-protective reaction. Although we know consciously that media images are only images, we feel fear when the ax murder is stalking the helpless woman. A young child can mistake such images for the real thing. In a documented case, a child hit a TV screen with a hammer because of the frightening images he saw.

The images of violence young people see on television, in the movies, and through video games can condition them to react as if life were full of actual threats to their physical well-being when, in fact, they are only being threatened mentally, psychologically.

That's not to deny that the world has some brutal and horrifying aspects, and that children need to be properly prepared to deal with them. But the constant playing and replaying of violent media images over time can lock children unnecessarily into an ongoing *psychological* fight-or-flight vision of the world as a constantly threatening place. They may also think that their physical survival is being challenged, when the challenge is only mental. This feeling that life is dangerous can itself be very dangerous, for it can motivate us to action just as the cheers of the crowd can motivate athletes to victory.

What the Martial Arts Can Do

It is human to want to either fight or run away in the face of threats. But what many of us do not know is that we don't *have to* respond either way. That's where Martial Arts for Peace come in. The martial arts can give a student the confidence to *not* react in this way. It can accomplish this by teaching students how to protect and defend themselves both physically and mentally. At the Martial Arts for Peace school, students are taught the various ways we are all conditioned, and then shown how to break the chains of that behavior. They are shown how the violent images they have been subjected to can mislead them to acting as if they were facing a real physical threat.

Once we understand how we are conditioned,
we can stop acting in conditioned ways.

These students are instilled with a great sense of power through discovering that they themselves do not have to be controlled by their conditioning. In order to free ourselves of a conditioned reaction, we have to *understand* that we are acting in a conditioned way. Then we can see that our brain has misinterpreted a psychological threat for a physical threat, which has primed us to react defensively.

Understanding and Coping with Fear

The Martial Arts for Peace school teaches students that fear is an underlying factor in any conflict we experience, whether that conflict is something we feel inside or happening to us outside, socially. Fear is a human emotion, and there is no shame in feeling it. In this violent world in which we live, we experience it every day. It is normal today to feel as if our survival is perpetually at risk, since we are continually bombarded by images of violence.

What effect does this have on us? We come to believe that conflict is a natural and necessary part of life, and our fear begins to feed on itself. Most importantly:

> *Fear conditions us to believe in the existence of the "enemy," and that "enemy" in turn causes us to fear.*

When you think of the word "enemy," what images does it conjure up for you? Our fears are deeply rooted, and may be visualized as an attack by an angry parent, an irrational neighbor, or a brutal police force. Our fears are not a local condition; the whole world seems to place us in jeopardy and the whole world in some way fears. In fact, even though the world is more peaceful now that in times past, its dangers, perhaps only because of better media coverage, appear to be deepening. Most Americans grew up considering Russians as the enemy; now, it seems, we are being taught to fear the North Koreans, the Chinese, and terrorists of all stripes. So we teach our children to meet the enemy defensively. We don't discuss differences; we prepare militarily.

Another commonly perceived threat is an economic one—the persistent precariousness of our financial well-being. We see others as competitors and we wage war through business. We promote our products aggressively, afraid that competitors will get to the market first. We pressure our children to get high grades, enter good universities, and land well-paying, prestigious jobs. It's as though we are biologically driven to be aggressive, to react to the world as an intrinsically dangerous place and thus to drive ourselves and our children to fight and to compete. Yet instead of quelling the dangers, our responses to the threats we perceive simply cause more pressure and violence. Consider the students who committed the terrible crimes described in the first chapter: They certainly had specific images of their "enemy." Where did those images come from? How did they begin?

Our tremendous energy to be aggressive derives, in part, from being constantly stimulated by the fight-or-flight mechanism. It is as though the mechanism has become fused, locked in the "on" position, and we are living out a continual adrenaline rush. Unable to run away, we fight—we grow more aggressive, more militant.

The Martial Arts for Peace school shows students where the concept of the enemy comes from and how we humans are psychologically conditioned to believe that such ideological opponents exist. In fact, we ourselves are the ones who create the image of our enemy. And once we understand this, we no longer need be victims of conditioning. We have the insight to understand for ourselves whether an image, a person, a group, or a nation is, in fact, the enemy we thought it to be.

Developing an Understanding of Self

While conventional martial arts today primarily focus on training of the body, at the Martial Arts for Peace school, students are trained both physically and mentally. Mental martial arts, properly executed, train the mind to be disciplined, to learn, to have the strength of character and presence of mind to be observant, aware, and questioning.

At the foundation of all martial arts is the issue of psychological and biological conditioning and the conflict they create. If we read the early history of the martial arts, we can see this issue being addressed. In my estimation, it is one of the most profound and valuable insights contained in the martial arts. This is why I belive that this component of conditioning—the understanding of the self, why we are the way we are—needs to be included in all martial arts training. Only when we develop an understanding of ourselves can we understand others. And only when armed with an understanding of both can we resolve conflict peaceably.

When we acquire through physical self-defense training the knowledge and confidence to cope with aggression, that is, a belief that we can defeat any perceived threat, we have in a sense "defused" our biologically conditioned fight-or-flight system. We are allowed the opportunity to respond rationally without this powerful defensive instinct interfering. We can now use our mental self-defense skills to get out of a potentially hostile situation; resorting to our physical self-defense skills becomes unnecessary. This seeming paradox—that one learns how to fight to prevent fighting—is the real value of physical self-defense training. Yet conventional martial arts do not teach students about their conditioned reaction or the mental skills to deal with aggression.

Consequently, the physical skills they teach serve only to reinforce fear, and thus justify the need to fight.

Without understanding the causes of conflict, the goal of all true martial arts, the martial artist possesses only physical self-defense skills that by themselves are dangerous.

This issue is dealt with in all my books, especially in those written for young people. Without being part of a complete Martial Arts for Peace program, physical skills lack an appropriate context, and may be harmful. Young people come to believe that physical skills alone can resolve conflict peacefully when, in fact, they can actually create *more* conflict.

- *The fundamental goal of the martial arts is to understand and avoid conflict* before *it becomes physical.*
- *Physical skills are taught to give students confidence to use mental skills instead of fighting.*
- *When students acquire both mental and physical skills, they have the ability to deal with conflict at all levels.*

There is no other activity, discipline, or philosophy I know that can address conflict at all levels. When parents, teachers, and martial arts instructors recognize this fact, the martial arts can take their proper place in society as a successful solution to the overwhelming problem of violence. People will be able not only to do something about conflict *after* it begins, but before it starts.

Understanding conditioning is the key to understanding human conflict. It is the key to understanding conflict at the core, in the human brain, *our* brain, in the way we think and act and how we become involved in arguments, physical confrontations, and war. It is vitally important that we understand conditioning if we are to have a peaceful world. If we don't turn this key and open the door to this whole solution to dealing with conflict, we have little hope of our children learning how to avoid or end it—peacefully, without fighting.

"Show me Your Black Belt"

A Story

I was teaching a workshop in New England, talking to a small group about how to use our brain instead of our brawn when confronting a bully, when a young man approached. Paying no attention to the fact that I was talking to others, and in the middle of a sentence, he rudely interrupted me and shouted, "Show me your martial arts!"

I turned to him and saw, in an instant, that he was a child, with little understanding of manners and a huge need to get immediate attention. I smiled at him and said, "I am showing you now."

He looked dumbfounded for a moment as I turned back to the others and went on explaining how to resolve conflict peacefully before it escalated into a fight. I suppose he was quite disappointed, having expected me to leap up in a flying kick and break a dozen boards.

His question, however, gave me an insight. I realized that the instructors at this school were adept at the physical aspect of martial arts training, but had little or no understanding of their mental dimension. Before my seminar they were practicing their forms and doing especially well in deference to me, the visitor who had come to observe them. They were quite a bit younger than I, and I had the feeling that perhaps they were showing the "old bull" what the young ones could do.

This particular school was large, with about five hundred students, and most were practicing when I arrived. I was sure that my seminar, scheduled to follow practice, would have a good turnout. About ten minutes later, however, most of them left; only a few parents and kids showed up to hear my talk on "How to Defeat the Bully the Smart Way." How sad, I thought, that there were so few. When all evidence shows that children need mental self-defense skills to resolve conflict peacefully, why do we just keep on teaching them how to punch and kick? Why don't we think about educating the minds of our students as well as their bodies?

The quality of participants who did attend the seminar, however, was very high. They all understood the necessity for learning mental skills as a way to cope with the urgent problem of bullying, and all had a strong desire to acquire such skills for themselves.

After the parents and children left, I spoke to the instructors alone. Inspired by the boy who had interrupted me earlier, I said to them, "Show me your black belt without doing anything physical."

They were surprised by the request. Then, as what I had said slowly dawned on them, I got angry stares. They knew exactly what I was talking about, but their minds were closed to accepting anything new.

I think such experienced martial artists probably realize the importance of some mental component of their practice, but don't know clearly what it is and are incapable of teaching it. It is too elusive and subjective, not flashy and obvious like the physical skills. It's difficult to demonstrate, therefore harder to impart, and even harder to judge.

CHAPTER 5

The Art of Mental Self Defense

Funakoshi Sensei, the founder of Shotokan Karate, said in his humble book, *Karate Do: My Way of Life*, that even a monkey can perform the physical skills of martial arts. Perhaps this seems a harsh statement, but I think that what he was trying to point out is that the martial arts are much more than physical self-defense skills. Funakoshi Sensei was also a school teacher and knew the value of education and how it also applied to the practice of the martial arts.

It is true that anyone with gymnastic or athletic talent can easily learn these physical self-defense skills. Knowing the ease with which such physical skills can be acquired, and knowing their limitations, why do the majority of martial arts classes continue to emphasize and glorify them only? Why don't they educate the mind as well as the body?

Looking at all the horrific martial arts, war, and action films that glorify the violent resolution of conflict, one would think that humans in fact prefer fighting to peace. Young people are taught history by memorizing the dates of battles and admiring the warriors who won them. Our children have been conditioned to think that fighting is the honorable, and perhaps only, solution to the resolution to conflict. This notion is deeply programmed into their psyches and is reinforced by the current portrayals in the media, in which "peaceful" people are depicted as weak and unsuccessful, as "wimps." The warriors in the media, especially in the cartoons for children, are depicted as mighty, valiant, almost godlike beings that are protecting us from "mega" enemies, enemies so mighty that it takes a superhuman being to conquer them. It is this warrior image that has prevailed in society and has been carried over to the general view of what a man (and now a woman) should be. It is no wonder that the martial arts have become what they have, conditioned by the same admiration of toughness and belligerence.

We say we want our children to be kind, sensitive, and peaceful, but I believe many parents feel that for their children to be safe and to be successful in this dangerous world, they must be tough and combative. They must be "warriors" to succeed, to become wealthy and powerful, to make their mark in a hostile world. We are conditioned to view peace as ineffectual, therefore undesirable. We give lip service to the appreciation of people of peace but underneath that false veneer most of us prefer our children to be ambitious and aggressive. Consciously or unconsciously, the martial arts are seen by many people as a means to accomplish that end. They do not turn to the martial arts as a means for peaceful resolution of conflict, nor even a means for training young people to defend themselves. The real goal is having their children be competitors, be winners. Earning a black belt is a relatively quick way for people to be recognized. It is a shortcut to notoriety in a Hollywoodized society that thrives on pop successes. It is a way for people who feel they are nobodies to be a somebodies. You can look in any big city *Yellow Pages* under "martial arts" and see what kind of people they wish to attract by seeing what their ads promise. The "promises" I listed at the beginning of Chapter 2 were copied straight out of a phone book.

In Defense of Physical Martial Arts Skills

On the other hand, there are some well-meaning people who reject the conventional "warrior" approach of martial arts, and because of this reject the value of martial arts training entirely. Afraid that martial arts can only teach their children violent ways of dealing with the world, they throw out the baby with the bath water. This is unfortunate, but is a direct result of the sad state of most martial arts training today. Most of us in martial arts have simply not had the right training. We have not understood the real potential these excellent arts have in helping people resolve conflict peacefully.

The first impulse a child feels when threatened is a self-protective fear, and the most common response, as we now know, is either to fight or run away. Most of us humans think in this same either/or way. But why let our children continue to think that these are their only alternatives when there is so much more they can do? When children know physical self-defense skills, they have the confidence to *not fight* a bully, and to *not run away* from a bully.

The greatest potential of the martial arts is to help our children learn that peaceful behavior is created by understanding what prevents it.

Physical self-defense can give students more power over their instinctive conditioned reactions by teaching them physical ways to defend themselves. Knowing these ways gives students the confidence to consider carefully other appropriate, nonphysical, responses to potentially threatening situations. Instead of being at the mercy of their biological instinct, they are trained to use their minds—to focus and to think for themselves.

"I don't have to fight," they can think to themselves. "Although this bully is tall and strong, I don't have to run away. Maybe I can make friends. Maybe I can use humor and make him laugh. Maybe I can get help." Physically trained in the martial arts, a student feels physically competent. Then, when confronted by a threat of any kind, the student can center his or her thoughts on what to do to avoid the conflict. Rather than worry about fighting or running away, the student focuses on *preventing* a fight.

Mental Self-Defense Provides Perspective

Improper mental conditioning creates a "fixed" perspective, a habitual way of reacting, or a rock-hard, unchanging, established state of mind. This kind of mental conditioning—training someone to think in rigid patterns of thought and behavior—is in fact brainwashing. It is destructive, individually and socially. In the physical practice of martial arts, it affects the student's ability to respond correctly to an attack. When students engage in a freestyle competition, for example, they have no idea know what their opponent or counterpart is going to do; they must be prepared to face any possible type of threat. If they have a fixed, habitual way of reacting, they will be easily beaten.

Training our children to think in fixed, rigid ways works in the same, counterproductive manner. Do we want our children to respond in rote ways, or do we want to arm them with choices so that they can choose for themselves the right way to respond in any given situation?

ARMing Our Children with Knowledge

As a concerned parent, I want to help arm our children—with knowledge—to help them cope with conflict at all levels. The way Martial Arts for Peace accomplishes this combines insights from the fields of education, psychology, and the martial arts. Together they form a complete, revolutionary new approach that can train young people in two ways. Martial Arts for Peace:

- *Teaches children how to deal with bullies* without *resorting to violence.*
- *Teaches bullies how to get what they want* without *resorting to aggressive behavior.*

Many people believe that combining mental skills, which help us peacefully resolve conflict, with physical skills, which give us the ability to defend ourselves, is a contradiction. But years of experience have shown me that when children can make use of physical and mental skills together, they can be taught to understand and avoid conflict.

As I have already said, but perhaps bears repeating, is that physical self-defense skills give young people a necessary self-assurance. They feel confident because they know they are able to defend themselves if they need to. This creates an inner sense of power. However, this ability to defend themselves is a skill they must use only *after* the conflict already exists—after the threat of physical confrontation is already there.

The intention of teaching young people both the physical and mental skills of martial arts is to help them to stop conflict *before* it starts—to avoid and therefore prevent it. I cannot say enough times:

The true goal of the martial arts is to stop conflict before it begins.

When conflict cannot be prevented, we need to know how to resolve it. Once the conflict exists, what can we do to untangle the knot? When it cannot be resolved, we need to know how to manage it. Now that it exists and it's gotten out of hand, what do we do to stop it?

Acquiring the skills to deal with conflict at all these levels is life-changing, because it provides our children with options. They don't have to fight. They don't have to run away. A gap is created, in which they can think and then act, not react. My complete, three-point program for dealing with conflict, introduced earlier, can be summarized in the abbreviation **ARM**.

Avoid conflict, by understanding its causes and therefore actively preventing it. Learn to be aware of the "body language" of potential aggressors. What messages are they sending you by the way they walk, talk, or look at you? Also beware of your feelings about a situation. What "vibes" are you picking up? Trust your instincts. Thinking even more deeply, try to understand what motivates a person to want to bully you. Then you are understanding the causes and not just reacting to the symptoms.

Resolve conflict, by learning mental self-defense skills through roleplaying and using nonviolent alternatives. Verbal skills allow you to talk your way out of a potential conflict. It is using your brain instead of your brawn. The bully has one purpose—to hurt you emotionally or physically. You can learn how to resolve conflict, at this level, by using mental martial arts. These skills are useful for the whole of your life and all your relationships.

MANAGE CONFLICT, BY LEARNING PHYSICAL SELF-DEFENSE SKILLS WHICH GIVE YOU THE CONFIDENCE TO *NOT* FIGHT. When you learn how to protect yourself physically, you feel confident that you can handle a fight if it comes to that. But more importantly, learning how to defend yourself gives you the confidence not to freeze up, not to be so afraid that you must either fight or run away. Running away can be an intelligent alternative, but it should be done with confidence.

Creating a Gap

Let's say that a child is approached by a hostile-looking bully. Just the menacing look of the bully can stimulate the child's fight-or-flight reaction. But just because the bully looks hostile doesn't necessarily mean that he or she is going to attack. When we react in a defensive, self-protective manner to a supposed threat, we are inhibiting an appropriate response to the actual situation. Is this bully an enemy or not? If we are trapped unnecessarily in a fight-or-flight reaction because we *think* we may be picked on, we are limited in what we can do; we are reacting to a perceived, psychological threat to our well-being. *The key is to be aware of what is really going on.*

If our fight-or-flight instinct is always in operation, we need to break that pattern of instinctive response.

The point is to have the confidence to step back from fear, to actually observe what it is, to create a "gap," a place where fear gets temporarily suspended. This gap is a space that is created in the primitive fight-or-flight mechanism that is our instinctive survival reaction. When our fear is in a state of abeyance, our mind is free to explore intelligent alternatives to the situation. We can respond to the specific situation at hand; rather than react in a habitual, fearful manner, we can act with intelligence. Feeling confident in our physical skills, our minds are clear to focus on the conflict itself.

The Martial Arts for Peace Way

- *Our children learn how to defend themselves physically, so they feel confident.*
- *Feeling confident, they are not trapped in a fight-or-flight reaction.*
- *Their minds are focused and clear so that they can use their first two lines of defense—which is to avoid conflict or to resolve it without resorting to physical means.*
- *They can reason their way out of a potential conflict instead of fighting or running away.*

This is the best of both worlds, the best combination of brawn and brain, muscle and intelligence, the balance between brute force and reason. By learning mental self-defense, learning to use the most powerful muscle in their bodies—their brains—our children acquire the skills to prevent conflict by employing nonviolent alternatives instead of resorting to brute force, getting hurt physically, running away, or feeling emotionally hurt.

These nonviolent alternatives can be instrumental in stopping violence before it starts. They are powerful tools. But we have to have them at hand when we need them, which means that they must be practiced regularly.

Twelve Ways to Walk Away with Confidence

Here are twelve ways that we and our children can learn to use in tough situations to allow us to walk away with confidence. They can be fun, and they can be life-saving. Use this chart when you're planning activities at home. Practice makes close-to-perfect.

1. **Make Friends.** Treat the bully as a friend instead of an enemy.

2. **Use Humor.** Turn a threatening situation into a funny one.

3. **Walk Away.** Don't get into it. Just walk away.

4. **Use Cleverness.** Use your imagination to resolve the conflict.

5. **Agree with the Bully.** Let insults go without fighting back.

6. **Refuse to Fight.** The winner of a fight is the one who avoids it.

7. **Stand Up to the Bully.** Stick up for yourself. Just say NO! to bullying.

8. **Yell!** A powerful shout can end conflict before it starts.

9. **Ignore the Threat.** Like bamboo, bend in the wind. Don't give in to revenge.

10. **Use Authority.** Call a teacher or adult to help you end the conflict.

11. **Reason with the Bully.** Use the most powerful tool you have—your brain.

12. **Take a Martial Arts Stance.** Be a victor, not a victim.

The Need for Conflict Education

Most of us wish violence would go away. But we cannot avoid it by pretending it doesn't exist. Perhaps we feel that it can't happen to *our* children, but it can, and it does. The first thing a parent says when it does is, "Why me?" "Why didn't we prepare ourselves?" When we ARM our children with conflict-prevention skills, we can feel confident that they are developing *total* skills and that we are doing everything we can to help them successfully cope with conflict and bullying in a peaceful manner.

In order to ensure that this opportunity is available for our children, we need to actively support this type of education. And why wouldn't we support education that has the potential to create a safe and peaceful world for them, for their children, and for generations to come? Conflict education consists of skills that need to be taught if the martial arts are to progress beyond being a physical self-defense, a sport and exercise regime. Karate or Taekwondo may work up a great sweat, but they do nothing to protect your child from violence if not taught as whole arts.

Today, because more young people have access to lethal weapons, physical self-defense skills are severely limited as a means of self-protection.

What good are physical self-defense skills against a gun? With mental self-defense skills, young people have a better chance to survive a conflict situation—by working to resolve the conflict before it gets to such an intense level that someone feels the need to use a deadly weapon.

Considering the many recent incidents of school violence, the need for conflict-education programs are obviously of paramount importance. Yet, most martial arts schools, places that could successfully address this urgent issue, have not participated in formulating solutions. Why is it that, while more and more parents, school teachers, administrators, law enforcement officers and counselors are recognizing the need to help young people address conflict nonviolently, martial arts schools continue to offer only conventional self-defense skills? Why teach only one level of defense—the physical—when we can ARM our children to the three levels of conflict education? Our overall goals in imparting conflict-education skills can also be summarized in the easily remembered three **P**'s:

Prevent. Help young people avoid conflict through awareness training.

Prepare. Give them verbal self-defense skills to allow them to resolve conflict peacefully, before it gets physical.

Protect. Give them the confidence to manage a potentially hostile situation by teaching them physical self-defense skills.

A Totality of Skills

I therefore advocate that children participate in martial arts training but only if their school offers *all* levels of conflict education. As we have already discussed, teaching a child only physical responses does not resolve conflict in a world of deadly weapons. But that goes for mental skills, too. To teach a child "conflict resolution skills" alone, which can be used only after the situation has become a conflict, is to miss the point. Intellectual skills by themselves do not give the child the confidence to cope with the basic primal fear he or she feels when being bullied.

After many years of successfully working with young people, it is my view that combining all levels, teaching children intellectual as well as physical skills, gives them the totality of skills needed to address bullying or any other violence that occurs in relationships. If the first two levels—prevention and preparation—are taught properly, a child may never have to resort to protection via physical means.

As we have discussed, our natural instinct when threatened by a potential aggressor is to fight or run away. When a properly trained martial artist is threatened by a potential aggressor, that instinct is held in check by reason. The first questions the trained martial artist asks is, "How can I reason my way out of this conflict without fighting?" "How can I keep this conflict from escalating without running away?"

Of course, there is a temptation for all martial artists to use the physical skills they have practiced. They want, quite naturally, to know if their training has worked. But the proper response is not to react according to instinct, but to act based on learned mental skills. Martial Arts for Peace teaches them to think, "I know I have physical skills to deal with this bully, but is it possible for me to use restraint—and *not fight?*" "Is it possible for me to *stop* this conflict? To *prevent* a fight?"

Conflict is not an either/or situation, requiring fight or flight! Physical skills give a student the confidence to not fight, and mental skills give the student peaceful means to resolve the conflict. It's as easy as that!

Using Roleplaying to Practice Mental Skills

Roleplaying can be very effective in helping us work out our fears. Play-acting, or acting out situations of potential conflict, also enables us to practice using nonviolent alternatives. When young people "play out" these situations, they often understand the information they need to learn more easily. When young children are playing house, taking the roles of Mommy and Daddy dolls, it is not an unproductive activity. They are discovering what it is like to be a mother or father. They are roleplaying parents.

When students roleplay a bully or a victim, they are learning first-hand what it is like to be each of those people. Their understanding grows deeper. The main objectives of roleplaying are:

To create a safe, controlled, and supportive atmosphere, where young people can act out threatening situations. This can relieve the pressure and anxiety about conflict they may be experiencing.

To offer the chance to create alternatives actions in encounters with conflict, creating a sense of power and confidence that can carry over into actual threatening situations.

To give the young person a chance not only to play out the role of the victim, but also to play out the role of the bully. This gives the student the opportunity to walk in the other person's shoes, to better understand why that person would want to be a bully. This helps relieve fear and promotes a more subjective, empathetic understanding of another person's plight.

To help young people become more aware of their own contribution to the problem, by creating, recreating, or re-enacting a disruptive event.

To give young people an opportunity to see how he or she would have prevented the situation from happening in the first place.

Two Methods of Roleplaying

Through roleplaying, young people have the opportunity to create their own alternative responses to conflict situations. Most roleplays have a bad guy and a good guy, a bully and a victim. Neither party is truly all good or all bad in real life, but when we start with a black and white situation, it helps us learn about the grays. Two type of situations that can be used to set the scene for roleplaying are:

Real-Life Situations. Using true-life situations may cause very real emotional trauma to be uncovered. Real-life situations hit home, and students may have strong emotional reactions to them. Such emotions, however, usually help motivate them to understand and want to do something about the problem.

Made-up Situations. When students or teachers make up situations, roleplaying seems only play-acting, so delving deeply into real emotional problems is less likely. However, an advantage is that the "distance" it has from real life encourages participation by those for whom roleplaying a real-life conflict situation might be too traumatic.

Learning Mental Self-Defense through Roleplaying

When we roleplay conflict situations, I ask for volunteers. I tell the roleplayers what the roleplay is about and sometimes hand out sheets that have roleplays already written out for them to read.

Other times I have the children create their own roleplays, based on real situations or made-up ones. I ask them to use at least one nonviolent alternative they have recently learned. The children are very creative and always amaze me with their ingenuity. It is play for them, but they also learn nonviolent alternatives far more quickly and easily when they can roleplay them.

After roleplaying, and sometimes during it, I ask the students, "Which alternative is the bully using?" "Which nonviolent response is the victim using?" In real-life situations, I stay in control of the game. I allow them to freely and independently explore their feelings and situations, but I am there for them, if they need help.

Roleplaying helps young people resolve conflict before it starts by using mental self-defense skills instead of physical ones. This exercise stimulates thinking. In Chapter 8 are roleplaying examples which you can use in the comfort of your own home. They are learning devices for everyone in the family and a fun way to spend family time.

CHAPTER 6

Teaching the Act that Conquers Fear

Why do we say, "Please," "Thank you," or "May I?" Are these just words we have been taught to use to appear polite or well bred? What do these words say about us? How do you feel when you hear them? How do you feel when they come out of your mouth or the mouth of your child?

Polite language is a component of good manners, a form of habitual social behavior that people engage in according to prevailing customs. In some societies, levels of polite language are used to indicate social position. In modern democratic societies we view manners more simply, as proper behavior, actions that show our regard for other people and the things that belong to them. Nevertheless, manners are sometimes difficult to teach young people.

In the study of martial arts, the definition of manners goes beyond social customs, and our reasons for using them go beyond a desire to express our good upbringing and respect for others.

The most sensible and appropriate manners have always been based on the Golden Rule: "Do unto others as you would have them do unto you." If we want others to treat us well, we need to treat them well. It is a matter of give, and you will get. When someone is kind to us, we are likely to treat that person kindly. People all over the world, no matter who they are or what they do, want to be treated with kindness and respect.

Fear Can Dissolve Respect

When we get into situations that frighten us, we can easily forget our manners. When we meet someone who appears threatening, or when someone says something that hurts our feelings, we can easily forget to act with respect—toward ourselves as well as others. If someone we know acts dishonestly towards us, our respectful feelings may vanish, and we may act upon our negative thoughts. We forget sometimes, when meeting people who are different from us, to act kindly and politely toward them. Sometimes, caught up in our own hopes and desires, we forget to share time with others; we usurp it all, focusing only on ourselves.

Whether working, playing, or just being with other people, there are usually circumstances in which we forget to look outside ourselves and notice how others are doing, whether we are treating them well, or whether they need our help.

Why bother to learn manners? Is it a matter of getting our children to obey us? Do we believe that getting them to learn manners will make them more controllable? Easier to teach? Better people? Is using manners the difference between a child who is good and one who is bad?

The Advantage of Mutual Respect

Perhaps you and I were taught manners at home because our parents believed that poor manners would reflect on them and their ability to bring up children properly. They worried about how other people saw them. Or perhaps our parents used manners as a way to reward or punish us. These reasons cannot, and most likely will not, motivate children today.

At the Martial Arts for Peace school, the focus on manners is more constructive, less punitive. There is one basic purpose for using manners in our lives and it has nothing to do with good or bad, reward or punishment. That purpose is: to live in loving and intelligent relationships with people around us—those we know as well as those we don't know—so that everyone shares mutual respect.

We teach our students that manners help us feel good about ourselves, as well as about others.

Rather than consider manners as what we should do, manners should be what we want to do. Along with developing our physical strength and sharpening our mental prowess, improving our manners is a desired goal.

We also teach that when we express our thoughts, feelings, words, and actions in a loving, intelligent, respectful way, we are less likely to feel conflict inside ourselves. When we feel less conflict within, we are less likely to generate conflict without, or get into it with other people. By learning and using manners, we live by a martial arts code of conduct and practice attaining its greatest achievements.

Respect is the act that conquers fear. When we respect our own thoughts and actions and those of other people, we put ourselves in the frame of mind that creates the "gap"—that space where fear is not dictating our actions.

Martial Arts for Peace Warm-ups

In the study of martial arts, warming up can help create that gap. Becoming loose and flexible makes one capable of responding to the moment with alertness and creativity. It is an engaging of the whole person, recognizing that the goal is to respond intelligently to life.

Effective classroom warm-ups should challenge students both mentally and physically, and they need to reflect the goal of teaching respect. The following warm-ups are used in Martial Arts for Peace schools, and you may want to think about ways to use them at home.

Warm-up 1. Children are asked to line up their shoes in an orderly fashion by the door. This brings their attention to the present, preparing them to be aware of the lesson of the day.

Warm-up 2. The frame of mind of students is very important. The young ones, especially, may appear anxious and "antsy," so it is good to have them begin with an easy, fun physical activity. One such exercise is running around in a circle while the instructor tells them to stop or go, run sideways or backwards. In this way, the young students are given an opportunity to work out their daily frustrations in an energetic way before the regular class begins.

WARM-UP 3. The students begin with physical warm-ups but do them with a twist. Instead of going though their regular warm-ups in a mechanical way, it is done within a game such as "Sensei Says" (like "Simon Says"). In this game, students have to be particularly attentive to what is going on. The basic goal is to train them to be alert.

WARM-UP 4. It is important to warm up their brains as well as their bodies. So, ample time is given to educating them about the true essence of the martial arts, avoiding and resolving conflict peacefully. To do this properly, an instructor needs the proper resources and training to provide students with the ability to understand, avoid, and resolve conflict without having to resort to physical means.

WARM-UP 5. Students are talked with about how their martial arts training relates to their lives outside the martial arts school—at home, in school, and within their community. This exercise warms up their social consciousness, as well as their innate sense of discipline, order, and respect.

The word "education" comes from the Latin word *educare,* which means "to draw out." Martial arts is not a method of conditioning young people to obey commands unquestioningly, but rather to "draw out" of them their natural sense of living intelligently. Our ultimate aim as martial arts educators is to help our students be intelligent, kind, and compassionate human beings, capable of relating to the challenges of daily life with dignity and understanding.

Teaching Goal Setting

What does it mean to have a goal? How do we set a goal? How do we teach our children the importance of goal setting? Goal setting is to have an end in mind. We need to be clear about our expectations and what the outcome of a situation will be. We need to "begin with the end in mind."

Step 1. The end results are evaluated What are they and how do they relate to the welfare of the group and, at the same time, of each individual student?

Step 2. End results are put to a "reality check." Are the expectations realistic? Are they up-to-date with the times? Are they outmoded for young people today?

Step 3. The goals are questioned as to whether they are helpful to the student in the broadest sense. In other words, can each student comprehend the "whole" of the martial arts, the mental aspects as well as the physical? This means that they should know what the martial arts can offer society, especially their ability to foster healthy relationships.

Step 4. Work is done to give students the right tools to achieve the set goals. The curriculum needs to encompass teaching them how to be proficient, not only in physical self-defense but also in mental self-defense. Will they learn how to avoid physical aggression by creative, nonviolent, nonphysical means?

Step 5. Students are given the necessary time to attain those goals, recognizing that these goals require a lifetime process of learning, and that individuals learn at different speeds. The basis of any martial arts practice is to prepare students for life, giving them not only the desire to attain a goal but the skills and resources to succeed.

Time and again, at the Martial Arts for Peace school, children are taught that respect is an act that can conquer fear. When children learn to respect themselves and others, to honor their thoughts and feelings as well as those of other people, their mental skills strengthen, and their confidence soars.

The Goals and Foundations of the Martial Arts for Peace

These considerations make up the goals of the program taught at the Martial Arts for Peace school. They also make up the foundation for a healthy and happy life.

Courtesy	Being well-mannered and considerate.
Gentleness	Living with affection and compassion.
Honesty	Being truthful.
Humility	Acting without self-importance.
Intelligence	Understanding what prevents peace.
Kindness	Caring for others as you would like to be cared for.
Love	Being a martial arts champion for peace.
Order	Being aware of what creates disorder.
Respect	Honoring the dignity of all life.
Responsibility	Meeting life's challenges with a courageous spirit.
Wisdom	Living without fear.

CHAPTER 7

Looking Toward the Twenty-first Century

The martial arts are at a critical stage in their evolution, a turning point that will determine in what direction they will go. Will they continue to flourish into the twenty-first century, or will they die out from over-commercialization and a limited potential? Are the martial arts just a fad fueled by exploitative Hollywood action films and media hype, or do they have an important and urgent role to play in society, especially in the education of our children?

The media in particular have presented the martial arts as skills that inflict violence and destruction. When they portray these skills as aggressive, superhuman gymnastic feats, they distort the real intention of these potentially peaceful and educational arts. They falsely represent the intent of martial arts to impressionable young people, who emulate what they see without the ability to differentiate between what is true or false. This view of martial arts practitioners as "warriors" is, unfortunately, the one generally accepted by young people.

The direction the martial arts will take for the twenty-first century depends on the vision we create. We can either continue to present this violent portrayal, and hence perpetuate the violent emulation of that behavior, or we can create a new vision—a Martial Arts for Peace vision—that places the martial arts in their proper place in society, as unique educational tools for the betterment of humankind.

Going Beyond Academics

Traditional public and private schools are primarily concerned with educating young people vocationally, with a focus on academic achievement. In order to meet today's urgent personal and social challenges of increased violence and the deterioration of ethical values, we need a different education, beyond the teaching of academics, one that can teach our children the skills to resolve conflict peacefully and build excellent moral character. If properly taught, the martial arts can be this education for peace and social good.

To be able to meet this obligation, martial arts schools of the twenty-first century will need highly trained Martial Arts for Peace educators who have the necessary skills and resources to prepare their students to cope with these challenges. New Martial Arts for Peace training programs and innovative curriculums will need to be developed in the evolution of these arts from self-defense skills and competitive sports to their greater potential of peaceful and spiritual disciplines, so that students and teachers can address the social ills of humankind.

With proper training in the Martial Arts for Peace, we can begin to do something about the violence and immoral behavior that is overwhelming our society. We want our children to be doctors, scientists, and engineers. Don't we also want them to know how to nurture peaceful relationships in their lives? Why can't we offer students a safe and controlled learning environment to explore warlike feelings within themselves?

Creating a Vision

Martial Arts for Peace can teach the virtues of compassion, love, wisdom, and respect, fine qualities that build strong and honorable character in young people. Then our children can contribute to the creation of a more peaceful, gentle world. The original Martial Arts of Peace—that became, over time, the Arts of War—have the transformative potential to again be peaceful and healing arts, but only with the right vision and the right means to carry out that vision.

Recognizing this evolving mission, we teachers and students of these arts must open our hearts and minds to a greater potential. If the martial arts are going to evolve into the new millennium and be an intelligent and effective force in the creative transformation of society, then that is what we need to envision. What we think is what we create. Our thoughts are what make the world, for better or for worse.

Some martial artists will limit their vision and stay safely within the conventional confines of what they have been taught. Others, especially Martial Arts for Peace educators, will create a new and bold vision to evolve and keep alive the peace and good will within these arts.

The martial arts are at a very important stage in their evolution from primarily physical endeavors to more complete systems, and this is the direction they will need to go to meet the needs of young people today. We need to help young people become respectful human beings, to get respect by giving respect, and to develop the strength of character needed to understand and resolve conflict peacefully.

Despite centuries of martial arts practice using both the physical and mental together, the work of the Martial Arts for Peace school in this day and age is a pioneering effort. It is a "renewed" frontier. It should be an integral part of every martial arts school worldwide, for it can enhance what is already being taught there. Moreover, it takes nothing away; it only enriches.

Why Relationship-Building Skills Are Essential

Violence and aggression are rampant in our society. Indeed, they are among the gravest dangers our children face growing up. Young people are victimized more than any other age group and experience an ongoing, significant risk of harm. Although juveniles make up only one-tenth of the population, they are victims in one out of every four violent crimes.

Why are schools experiencing a proliferation of violence? The most recent statistics from the Department of Justice indicate that twenty-five percent of children are fearful of being attacked in school. Still, bullying is often dismissed as a serious problem by both parents and teachers. Many of the reputed bullies apparently feel like outsiders. They are not star athletes or school leaders but children who are out of the mainstream. They are unhappy, searching for their places, and they suffer ridicule. Like the children who have committed murder, each feels like "a nobody who desperately wants to be a somebody."

These students need to learn more than how to take an "eye for an eye," or to believe that "might is right," attitudes that have perpetrated violence for thousands of years.

We encourage our children to participate and succeed in academics and athletics because we recognize that these endeavors are important for their development and welfare. Learning how to develop the strength of character and the mental and physical skills to understand and peacefully avoid conflict, from qualified Martial Arts for Peace educators, is the greatest lesson they can learn. We love our children, and want to ensure their safety and help them build excellent moral character. That is why we need to support Martial Arts for Peace programs and schools that can provide such an education. We must consider our children's Martial Arts for Peace teachers not just as self-defense instructors or coaches, but as educators who have the ability to teach relationship-building skills. Today, when there seems never to be enough time for our children to learn these valuable skills, I am personally grateful that, for a very reasonable cost and time commitment, our children are able to receive such an incredibly valuable experience.

If you feel as I do, that this type of education is vitally important and that it has the potential to successfully address the problem of bullying and violence that our children face every day, then we must take steps to guarantee them the right kind of education, where they can get the total skills they require to peacefully understand and prevent conflict.

What Parents and Teachers Should Do

- *Regularly attend our children's Martial Arts for Peace school, just as we attend their academic school, to talk with the Martial Art for Peace educators about how our children are doing.*

- *Treat Martial Arts for Peace educators, along with parents and teachers, as team members in the overall education of our children.*

- *Help our children at home by reading with them constructive books about understanding conflict and the intelligent practice of the martial arts.*

- *Familiarize ourselves with the methods our children are being taught to avoid conflict. Review and emphasize the creative, nonviolent options they may need to employ in a threatening situation.*

Martial Arts for Peace is a complete endeavor, one that addresses all levels of conflict, and thus unlike any other program in existence. Consequently, the Martial Arts for Peace educators we need to make the program more widely available must be trained. We need to begin to train them now, so that they in turn can offer the training and resources needed to educate young people about the true goal of all martial arts, which is peace.

Self Understanding

Based on the conflict we see in today's action films, our impression is that the martial arts are generally violent. Many children who see these films have no power of discernment. They literally "take in" what they see. For this reason many well-intentioned people have proposed banning or restricting the viewing of violent television programs, video games, and films.

Don't you think that the film and television industries could develop exciting, educational shows that teach young people how to resolve conflict nonviolently and still have a high degree of entertainment value? Wouldn't your child, and all children, be interested in understanding themselves? Wouldn't they want to know how their fears keep them from responding to threats in a creative, nonviolent way? Wouldn't they want to know about the "gap" they can create between their fears and their confidence? Don't you believe that your children would want to know ways they can walk away from conflict with confidence—without fighting?

For students to advance in rank in the Martial Arts for Peace, they are tested not only on their physical skills but on their understanding of the art of living with intelligence and sensitivity.

All great accomplishments in life begin with a dream, a vision. But we have to be more than dreamers. We have to educate ourselves about what it takes to make our dreams a reality. Those visionaries who put their dreams into practice are the ones who elevate new visions to their rightful place. For the martial arts, that place is where we can educate our children in society, and teach them intelligent means to resolve conflict, build character, and create peace.

"The Master of Nothing"

A Story

The cloudless sky was endless blue. The wind's invisible breath moved the delicate willow tree branches in a slow, waving motion like a dancer's grass skirt gently sweeping the ground. The multicolored birds moved quickly from tree to ground, seeking whatever food the earth provided. The high noon sun felt warm on the white martial arts uniforms of the students as they sat attentively in front of their teacher and the one who was standing over him, challenging the older teacher to fight.

"I have come to challenge you to fight, to see who is the most powerful. I have won many tournaments, defeating all my opponents in full contact freestyle matches. I have been awarded the rank of Grand Master, and have been given many trophies for my skills as a fighter. I have heard you are a great master of the martial arts, a master of empty-handed combat. I want to challenge you to see who is the best," the young, powerful-looking man threatened the older teacher.

The older teacher sat still looking this challenger directly in his eyes, seeing beyond the threats, beyond the outward show of pride and physical strength, beyond the fear that was deeply hidden within this young man.

"You are no doubt a great fighter. I believe what you say. But I am not a fighter like you. My challenge is in understanding the Ancient Warrior within, defeating the enemy without fighting, not in combat with another. I am a master of nothing."

The younger one looked confused as the older man continued. "And I see that you are trying to be somebody, to prove yourself in combat with others. Yet I wonder if this is the real challenge? You have obviously trained hard and have been successful in the physical side of the martial arts. But is this all there is? Can one be called a master only knowing this?" the older teacher asked gently with an amused smile.

"Your words are brave," said the young challenger, " but can you back them up with action? You don't look like a master of the martial arts," he replied boldly.

"I will accept your challenge to freestyle," said the older one, "if you first accept my challenge, the challenge of a true empty-handed Master of the martial arts, the challenge of being empty, of being nothing. I offer you three tests to pass, to prove your understanding and skill as a real master. This will be the most challenging combat you will ever encounter."

The rough-looking young man declared in a very loud voice, "I'm not afraid of anything you come up with."

"Good! Let's begin," said the older one. He then began to speak suddenly and with such intensity that everyone was shocked by his outburst. "But I think you are already defeated by your ignorance. How can a bragging fool like you ever pass my test? You are much too proud and stupid to understand anything intelligent. Your muscles get in the way of your understanding. You think that being able to jump around like a monkey and do gymnastic acrobatics, flailing your arms and legs about, is mastering the martial arts. You are an arrogant showoff, and know nothing of what it means to be a master!"

The young challenger was stunned momentarily. Then his face became red and furious. His body began to tremble with rage. His eyes flared and his fists hardened into tight knots. He approached the older one.

"You dare to speak to me like this! Do you know who you are talking to? Do you realize that I could squash you like a bug, that I could defeat you with both hands tied behind my back, if I wanted to?" he screamed, almost uncontrollably, at the teacher. "I am the greatest fighter of all time. I could break you right here and now! How dare you insult me like that?"

Without hesitation, the teacher jumped up, simultaneously letting out a tremendous *kiai* (yell), sending the arrogant challenger stumbling backwards, tripping over himself and falling unhurt onto the soft grassy ground. The shocked young man looked up in a daze at the older teacher who stood, smiling over him.

"My, my," smiled the old teacher. "See how this empty-handed master has defeated himself," the teacher spoke calmly to the students and the downed challenger. "He doesn't seem to understand that he was only fighting himself and therefore lost the first test by his pride and the second test by his anger. How can he call himself a master of the martial arts if he can so easily lose a real contest in mental self-defense?"

In that moment, caught so suddenly and completely off guard, the young man saw himself as if he were looking through someone else's eyes. He saw the rage, the out-of-control threatening, the loss of inner composure and strength. He saw that the insults had thrown him, that his pride stood in the way of what this teacher was telling him, which was the hard reality of truth. He saw that he had been defeated by the image he had of himself as someone important. He now saw a frightened, boastful, inexperienced young man who had lost his dignity, who didn't understand anything except that he had spent his life mastering only one very small part of himself. He realized in that moment how powerless he really was in the face of this sudden understanding

"Now sir," said the old teacher, "do you understand? Can you see yourself truly through new eyes? Can you see—not what you think you should be, but what you actually are—without judgment, without thinking positively or negatively about yourself? Can you just see?" The older teacher spoke gently, quietly, as if reading the fallen challenger's mind, at the same time offering a hand up to the younger man.

It was as if they were all suspended eternally in the eye of a hurricane. The birds chirped from the trees, unaware of the human scene below them. The beauty of nature seemed so intense that every brilliant green blade of grass stood out in a broad field before them. It was as if a great dark cloud had lifted. There was a delicate lightness, a feeling of infinite well-being.

"Stop! Look! Listen!," the teacher spoke with great authority. "The third and greatest test is here, now. It is what are you aware of in this moment. And if you can speak of it, you fail."

Surrounded by the immense beauty of nature and the universe, the young man was overwhelmed with a feeling he hadn't felt for years. It was as if he were a child again, lost and unknowing in the joyful splendor of the endless moment. Who he was before—that bragging, foolish, arrogant young man—was no longer real, it no longer mattered. All that mattered was now before him, the glory of the natural world in all its infinite wonder.

"Enter here, enter here!" the teacher commanded with intense compassion and delight. "This is the real world. We need to wake up from our dreams, our fears, our self-important images that we have built up of ourselves and the world we think revolves around us. They are false pictures that fill our minds and hearts with darkness and suffering. Be as empty as a bottomless bucket. Let the flow of life move through you without holding on to anything. Hold life lightly and feel its delicate heartbeat as your own."

The teacher pointed to the land, the trees, the sky, and laughed wonderfully. "You are that, and that is you. Do not be fooled by the things of the mind, for they are illusions, mere shadows on the wall. The image, the shadow, is not the real thing. Enter the realness of life and let fall away what you think it is."

The teacher then pointed to a bush of honeysuckle, a sweet cluster of small yellow flowers and said to the young man, "Enter there, and you will pass the test."

The young man did what he was asked. He bent over to smell the flowers and, as he did, he began to feel a great burden dissolve inside him. The sweet odor of the flowers filled his being, and there was only that. In that delicate moment, the living fragrance enveloped him. There was no one smelling the flowers. There was only the flower, the fragrance. He was gone, lost in that heavenly wonder.

"Now shall we fight?" a voice asked from afar.

"There is no need to now. There is nothing to prove, to fight against, except oneself. I am nothing, nobody, and so are you," he heard himself say, as if he were far away and yet, at the same time, deeply within himself and everything. The reply was himself, the birds, the sky and the teacher who spoke to him.

"You have passed the test," said the older one. "You are indeed an empty-handed master, a master of nothing. But the real test now begins. It is how you live your life from now on—how you treat other people and how you create peace in the world—that determines who and what you are."

CHAPTER 8

What Parents Can Do at Home

Growing up just outside New York city in the forties and fifties, my childhood was fraught with violence, As a result, I feel that teaching young people how to get out of potentially violent situations is just as important as giving them intellectual skills. The world at large can be a violent place, and young people must be educated about how to live peaceably in this time of great conflict. But there are fun, enjoyable ways to do this, and many of them can be done at home.

Inner Conflict Awareness Exercise

Conflict may not always be expressed by outward violence. Sometimes it surfaces as a simple disagreement with someone. Conflict inside us may remain there and fill us with inner pain, which commonly happens when our feelings have been hurt and nobody knows.

The following is an exercise in inner conflict awareness. It is important to understand the causes of conflict, how it starts, what makes it up. In this way we can end conflict before it gets to the expressive stage. Conflict often emanates from our conditioned beliefs and attitudes, the "shoulds" that have been painfully programmed into us, usually through a system of punishments and rewards. The intent here is to begin to be aware of these conditioned attitudes without judging them. In this nonjudgmental awareness, one has the opportunity to not react based on them.

You or your child can do this activity alone, by writing down answers on paper, or it can be done with a group of from two to four people. When doing the activity with others, everyone can write down responses privately, then share them afterwards. (For those interested in more of such activities I have written a separate curricula for parents and teachers to help young people understand and resolve conflict peacefully. Please refer to the information at the back of this book.)

Inner Conflict Awareness Exercise

1. Write on a piece of paper, "I believe" and then write down whatever comes into your head first. Write ten different responses. (You can also photocopy a sheet with the numbers 1 through 10, each followed by "I believe," for all participants.)

2. Now write, "I don't believe," and again write down ten responses, whatever comes into your head.

3. Now write, "I should," with ten more responses.

4. Then write, "I shouldn't," with ten more responses.

5. Now try, "I believe in." Yes, ten times!

6. Then write, "I don't believe in." And yes, ten times.

If you are doing this with others, everyone can take a turn at revealing responses. Compare responses with other participants. Ask one another:

> Why do you believe . . . ?
>
> Why don't you believe . . . ?
>
> Why do you think you should . . . ?
>
> Why do you think you shouldn't . . . ?

What did you find out? Were some of your answers the same as those of the other people? Were some different? Were some opposite? Ask each other:

> Where do your beliefs, "shoulds" or "shouldn'ts" come from?
>
> Where did you first learn this belief? At home? At school? From a friend? From a relative?
>
> Do you think you were born with these beliefs, or do you think you learned them?
>
> Why do you think you were conditioned to believe these things?

Nonviolent Alternatives

By studying and making up situations that use these alternatives, you and your family can strengthen your relationships with one another, and increase those positive relationships that you all have outside your family. Here's a chance to be inventive, creative. Go over these alternatives with your children, and take turns being the reader and the one who figures out how to handle the situation. You and your child can learn a lot from one another.

Twelve Ways to Walk Away with Confidence

Let's review the strategies, first introduced in Chapter 5, that we and our children can use in tough situations to allow us to walk away with confidence. Here we will discuss them in a bit more detail, with some actual examples.

1. **Make Friends.** Treat the bully as a friend instead of an enemy. Imagine a bully approaching you on the street. What's the first thing that crosses your mind? Will you act on this first thought that has entered your mind? Name five ways you could treat the bully as a friend instead of an enemy. Make up situations, using the names of people you know or characters in the movies.

2. **Use Humor.** Turn a threatening situation into a funny one. Think of a threatening situation. What might terrify you and make you feel threatened? Now, without thinking, turn it into a funny situation in your mind. What would that funny situation be? Name five funny things you could say in this situation that would make you feel less threatened.

3. **Walk Away.** Don't get into it. Just walk away. Close your eyes and imagine a loud-mouthed bully walking up to you and demanding that you move out of his way. Now, imagine yourself not afraid! Imagine yourself calmly saying, "Sure," and just walking away. What are five thoughts you can run by your brain to make you feel peaceful in this moment?

4. **Use Cleverness.** Use your imagination to resolve the conflict.There are many ways to be clever. Some of them are noisy; some are quiet. Some are funny; some are not. Let's say a bully has just approached you and asked for all your money. What are five clever things you could say to the bully that would lessen the threat of the situation?

5. **Agree with the Bully.** Let insults go without fighting back. Imagine a bully yelling at you, insulting you to such an extent that you can feel rage begin to swell up inside you. (Become that bully. Really yell and insult the other person.) How good are you at letting the insults go? What can you do to keep your mind completely peaceful?

6. **Refuse to Fight.** The winner of a fight is the one who avoids it. Practice refusing to fight someone who demands that you do. What are five ways you can refuse to fight? What can you say? What can you do? How can you convince a bully that not fighting is winning the fight?

7. **Stand Up to the Bully.** Stick up for yourself. Just say NO! to bullying. It is frightening to stand up to a bully, but when you know that the bully is someone who has been a victim, too—otherwise he or she wouldn't be a bully to begin with—then you know that you can protest. You can just say NO! What are five ways you could stick up for yourself if you were threatened by a bully?

8. **Yell!** A powerful shout can end conflict before it starts. Do you know how to yell, really loudly? It's good to practice where no one will come running, or people will call the police! A good yell can catch a bully by surprise and throw him or her off guard.

9. **Ignore the Threat.** Like bamboo, bend in the wind. Don't give in to revenge. Bullies can say very hurtful things.

What are some thoughts run through your mind when this happens? When we understand that the bully feels hurt, too, we can create a "gap," and in that space, forgive the bully for being mean. What are five ways you can think of to not give in to feelings of revenge?

10. **Use Authority.** Call a teacher or adult to help you end the conflict. Calling an authority—a parent, teacher, or other adult—is not being a "stool pigeon," as many children believe. It has a higher goal, that of stopping a fight before it starts. Who are five authorities you could call, depending on where you are and what time of day it is?

11. **Reason with the Bully.** Use the most powerful tool you have—your brain. Make up your own potentially violent situations and talk about the different ways you can use your brain to reason with the bully. Name a bully you know, and talk about how you've succeeded or failed in reasoning with this person. Then, come up with new ways to deal with the same situations.

12. **Take a Martial Arts Stance.** Be a victor, not a victim. When all else fails, we can prepare for the worse. But if we do fight, we always wonder afterward if there wasn't one more thing we could have done to prevent a fight. So, think preventively. See if you can come up with one of those ways first.

Roleplaying

For those of you who enjoy acting out parts, there is roleplaying. You and your children can play the roles already written for you, or you can make up your own. We've included roleplays from some of our materials that students have found to be fun and informative.

Before each roleplay, make sure everyone understands who is playing what part. For example, in the roleplay that follows, there are two characters, Peanut and Hook. (It helps to make photocopies of the roleplays so that each person can read separately.) The full benefits of roleplaying come from really getting involved in the parts. Explain that the words in italics tell what the character is *thinking,* and should be read aloud by whoever is taking that part.

The following four role plays demonstrate simply, at the child's level, the difference between someone who is being picked on that (1) knows only physical self-defense skills, and is consequently confused about using these potentially lethal skills in a situation that does not warrant them, and (2) someone who is being picked on but knows martial arts mental self-defense, nonviolent alternatives to defeat the bully the smart way—without fighting.

Peanut has been studying martial arts with an instructor who teaches physical skills *only.* Peanut has learned many martial arts moves and can do them skillfully. However, he has not yet learned any mental martial arts skills.

After the roleplay, you and your fellow roleplayer can ask one another the following questions:

1. Peanut knows some martial arts moves. Was he able to stop the fight?

2. Using martial arts moves that you know, would you have been able to stop that fight?

3. Peanut, did you feel any control in stopping that fight?

4. Hook, did you feel any impulse to stop the fight? Were you even more inclined to fight? Why?

Here's the roleplay. Have fun!

"How Can I Stop this Bully"

ROLEPLAY ONE

PEANUT

Uh-oh. Here comes Hook, again. That big bully doesn't know that I've been studying martial arts. If he gives me any trouble, he's in for a big surprise.

HOOK

Well, well, well. If it isn't my little buddy, Peanut. (Walks up to Peanut and puts a heavy-handed arm on Peanut's shoulder.) Seems to me we made a deal last time we met and you haven't come through.

PEANUT

Leave me alone, Hook! I didn't make any deal with you!

HOOK

You were about to give me your money, when we got interrupted. Now hand over that money, punk.

PEANUT

You better watch out, Hook! I've never told you this, but I'm learning martial arts, and you could get hurt.

HOOK

(Grabs Peanut's shirt.) Hah! You gonna hurt me, squirt? You and who else?

PEANUT

(Breaks free and does a kick that throws Hook off balance.)

HOOK

Why you little punk! (Comes at Peanut with his fist clenched, pretending to smash him.)

Now, perform the next roleplay, with the same people playing the same parts. Again, it will help to have photocopies of the roleplay. Most bullies push other people around in order to protect themselves from getting hurt—physically, mentally, or emotionally. Notice, and ask your child to notice, how Hook bullies—what exactly he says and does. This time you will hear what Hook is thinking as well what Hook says. Afterward, ask each other:

1. Did this roleplay help you understand why Hook bullies people?
2. Did you like Hook any better than you did before?
3. Do you think Hook needs help?
4. What do you think would help Hook?
5. What would you do in that situation?
6. Would you feel a need to protect yourself too?
7. Do you think that if you didn't feel a need to protect yourself, you could act more intelligently?

"I'm Protecting Myself"

ROLEPLAY TWO

PEANUT

Uh-oh. Here comes Hook, again. *Maybe I made a mistake by telling him I know martial arts. But I'll use them if he bullies me!*

HOOK

Well, well, well. It's my little buddy, Peanut. *This guy is small enough for me to pick on, and he scares easily. Much different from my brother who beats up on me. I'll just beat up on Peanut and show this kid that I can be tough too!* I appreciate the money you gave me last week. Problem is, I need more.

PEANUT

(Calmly) Listen, Hook! We had a deal, and I completed my part of the bargain. *This guy could eat me alive. If I don't act tough, he'll just beat up on me and take my money. I better get out of here, fast.*

HOOK

You talk awfully big for a squeaky little guy, you know? *He's acting tough, but I can tell he's really scared. The martial arts stuff is baloney. Reminds me of my father—always bluffing and puffing and pretending to be something more than what he is.*

PEANUT

Do I try a kick or a punch? This guy is getting serious. I'm going to have to do something, or run away. If I run, he'll run after me and that will fuel his fire even more. How do I get out of this?

HOOK

(Grabs Peanut's shirt.) You better pay up, or you are mincemeat!

For the following roleplay, about someone who knows mental martial arts skills, you will need three participants: Rusty, Topper, and Mr. Wood. Read aloud the words in italics, which tell you what each person is thinking.

In this roleplay, the person being bullied will use mental skills and hopefully not have to use physical ones. Watch for how many physical and how many mental skills are used. Afterward, ask one another:

1. Did you see physical skills? Mental skills? What kind?

2. Did Rusty trick Topper? Did Rusty really have money? Did Rusty have poison oak? Did Rusty call for help?

3. Do you think it was cowardly for Rusty to call for help? Didn't Rusty succeed in attaining the highest martial arts goal, which is to stop a fight?

4. Could you see the wheels turning in Rusty's mind as used mental skills to keep Topper from either hitting or taking money?

5. Do you see how possibilities open up to you when you can use mental skills?

"Can I Stop Conflict More Easily When I have Both Physical and Mental Skills?"

ROLEPLAY THREE

TOPPER

Boy, it looks like this kid has a lot of money. Look at those nice clothes. I wish I had that kind of money. Obviously , he has parents who care. Give me your lunch money!

RUSTY

(Looks at Topper and speaks calmly.) I don't have any money. I bring my lunch from home. *This is scary. I wonder if Topper can tell I'm using trickery. How do I get out of this type of situation without fighting? Take a deep breath and feel the scared feelings.* (Takes a deep breath.)

TOPPER

(Reaches out and grabs Rusty.) I don't believe you!

RUSTY

(Still speaks calmly.) Be careful! I've got poison oak! You could get it from me!

TOPPER

(Quickly lets go of Rusty.) I still want your money!

RUSTY

(Pretends to see a teacher coming.) Mr. Wood! Mr. Wood! We need help here! Topper needs some money!

MR. WOOD

You need money, pal? (Reaches into his own pocket.) I'll be glad to loan some to you for now. (Hands Topper some money.) I can also help you find ways to earn money, if you're interested and need it badly.

TOPPER

Yeah, I need it badly. What's it to you?

RUSTY

Mr. Wood, Topper's family is in trouble. He needs it. He'll pay you back, maybe my dad will hire him to mow our lawn or something.

Here's a final roleplaying situation, between two characters, Totem and Reggie. Again, read aloud the words in italics. Afterward, ask one another:

1. What skills did you notice being used?
2. If you were Reggie, the victim in this roleplay, how would you feel if the Bully demanded your homework?

3. As a Bully, what would you gain by getting Reggie to do your homework for you?

4. If you were Reggie, how would you feel about offering to help Totem to get the focus away from bullying?

5. Do you think it might make Totem, the bully, feel good to know that Reggie's heard he is a great basketball player?

6. Do you think someone like Totem could feel good about helping someone like Reggie? Why?

If you enjoy these roleplays and other exercises, the Martial Arts for Peace books and curricula contain a variety of games, exercises, and roleplays. You've no doubt heard that charity begins at home. At the Martial Arts for Peace school peace does, too.

"Hey, Brain"

ROLEPLAY FOUR

TOTEM

This kid always gets the teacher's attention; always knows all the answers. Schoolwork is hard for me; I don't like it when the teacher calls on me and I don't know the answers. No way I can please the teacher; I guess I must be dumb. No way to get the teacher's attention; I must be no good. Hey, Brain! Give me your homework!

REGGIE

(Looks at Totem.) *Oh, no. It's Totem again! How do I get rid of this bully?* I'd like to help you, but I already turned it in this morning.

TOTEM

You always get good grades, so you're gonna do my homework from now on, or else you're in big trouble.

REGGIE

I can't do your homework for you, Totem. It's not honest, for one thing. And you don't learn anything, for another. But I've got a better idea.

TOTEM

Okay, Brain. What's your brilliant idea?

REGGIE

I'll help you with your homework, if you do something for me. We'll make a deal.

TOTEM

Like what?

REGGIE

Let's meet after school today and talk. Maybe we can help each other. I hear you're pretty amazing at basketball. I'm lousy at it, so maybe you can teach me something.

APPENDIX

Questions and Answers with Dr. Terence Webster-Doyle

Parents, teachers, and children always have questions during the seminars we hold about Martial Arts for Peace, and after reading this book, you may have some as well. Below are those questions most frequently asked and my answers to them.

Q. Dr. Webster-Doyle, what is the main purpose of your work in the martial arts?

A. My goal is to make the martial arts a means by which people, especially young people, can learn practical skills to help them avoid and resolve conflict. The fundamental purpose of martial arts training is, and always has been, to resolve conflict peacefully.

Q. How is what you are doing different from what is now being taught in martial arts schools?

A. The martial arts are taught today primarily for self-defense, for fighting. I teach these same physical skills that other martial arts schools do; however, I emphasize the neglected "mental self-defense" aspect of the martial arts. Without these skills, students have only half of what they need to resolve conflict without having to fight.

Q. What makes you so interested in the martial arts? How do you see that they can help society?

A. The greatest challenge we have facing us today is violence in our relationships, in a word, bullying. It is our number one concern in society. It is epidemic and, according to the experts, it is going to get much worse unless we make a concentrated effort to prevent it.

Children are shooting each other in schools! How did we come to this? My concern is that we have allowed the problem to get to its worst stage. Then, after there's been a shooting, we rush in and try to patch things up through simplistic solutions like metal detectors. What happened this past year with school violence is an example of a growing trend. With my forty years of experience in the martial arts and conflict education, my feeling is that we can greatly reduce these terrible tragedies by teaching our children specific skills.

Q. What are these "mental self-defense" skills that you talk about? Is there any way you can state them simply?

A. The primary skill is to understand conflict—to identify it and to see immediately where it is coming from. When we can understand why it exists, we can then use our brain to come up with ways to avoid that conflict, and prevent it from happening. There are skills we can learn and practice that help us do this. We can also learn to resolve conflict by using nonviolent alternatives, especially verbal skills. The most powerful muscle we have is our brain. If we use it first, we may never have to use the other ones we have to fight.

Q. Why aren't our schools dealing with bullying?

A. There seems to be a denial by teachers and school administrators that bullying exists or is a serious problem. And for those who do recognize the problem, the solutions being offered are only partial, treating the symptoms. Partial solutions tend to be generally ineffective and can actually make the problem worse.

Q. It seems a sad commentary on our educational system that we are not helping our children learn the proper relationship skills to cope with all this violence. Do you personally feel that it is rather hopeless?

A. I don't think that it's hopeless. If I did, I wouldn't be doing what I do. I think that with the proper education, our children can learn how to avoid and resolve conflict peacefully, but first we need to awaken people, both children and educators, to the fact that this is possible.

Q. But if the schools aren't going to deal with this, where can our kids get these skills you're talking about? Can we teach them at home?

A. Some people think that I'm crazy to suggest this, but for me the perfect place to educate young people about these skills is in martial arts schools. I can understand objections to this, since most people only know martial arts through violent action films and video games. But when the martial arts are taught as a whole endeavor—presenting both mental and physical skills working together as one—then we have the opportunity to successfully prepare students to confront a potential bully.

Q. Do martial arts instructors have the background to teach both these skills? And what can they do about those who already are bullies?

A. The unique program we teach at the Martial Arts for Peace school—we call it ARM—combines insights from education, psychology, and the martial arts to form a revolutionary new approach that completely, wholly, trains young people how to cope with bullies. It also teaches bullies how to get what they want without resorting to violence. When bullies discover that they can have power without being violent, their perspective changes.

Q. Can you explain how ARM works?

A. **ARM** stands for: **A**void, **R**esolve, **M**anage. There are three levels of dealing with conflict. The first is to **A**void it, so that conflict in fact never begins. Children can be taught to understand and avoid being bullied when they have the physical and mental skills to do so. When they can avoid being bullied, they can prevent a fight. The intention of my program is to, whenever possible, stop conflict before it has a chance to begin—in other words, avoid it.

The second level is the **R**esolve stage. At this stage conflict exists, so let's try to resolve it. Many people think it a contradiction that one can mentally resolve conflict by combining it with a physical self-defense. But knowing how to defend themselves physically gives young people the confidence to defend themselves through other, nonphysical means.

The third level, to **M**anage conflict through physical self-defense skills, is taught so that the young person has the confidence to cope with potential aggression without "freezing," without reacting according to the very human fight-or-flight mechanism. We all know this reaction. When we're scared, we feel we either must fight or run away. Knowing how to defend themselves physically gives students the ability to use their brain first, to explore nonviolent alternative possibilities. The brain is our first line of defense. At this level, the conflict has already begun, so the challenge is to resolve it without resorting to physical means.

Q. So, you're saying that children have a better chance of protecting themselves if they use their minds instead of their bodies?

A. By combining physical and mental self-defense, our children learn physical skills to protect themselves but, at the same time, mental skills to employ nonviolent alternatives. Confident in their physical skills, they can choose nonviolent verbal skills to reason their way out of a potential conflict. This is a balanced combination of brawn and brain, the combined power of muscle and intelligence, a balance between brute force and reason.

Q. Do I understand you correctly when I say that your intent is to have our children use their brains first—but knowing physical self-defense skills clears their heads of worry. They know they can "handle" an opponent, but they focus on not having to?

A. That's absolutely right. Through learning mental self-defense, learning to use the most powerful muscle in their bodies, their brains, children have the skills to avoid conflict. They can employ nonviolent alternatives instead of resorting to the limited and dangerous alternative of brute force. Then they don't have to possibly get physically bruised, or run away, or feel emotionally hurt. They can learn to talk their way out, make friends with a bully, use humor, call a proper authority, ignore threats, or simply refuse to fight and walk away.

Q. I can see how a balanced program of physical and mental self-defense might lessen the potential for violence. Do you think martial arts schools will adopt this approach in the future? Will they want to design their programs to include what you are talking about?

A. More and more martial arts instructors are recognizing the need to teach all the skills we are talking about. They see that physical skills alone are not enough. They know that if their schools are going to survive, they are going to need programs like Martial Arts for Peace that successfully address what to do about bullying and other acts of violence.

They know that parents, teachers, counselors, and school administrators are recognizing the need for conflict-education programs that give young people the ability to protect themselves. Many inner-city schools have already begun teaching conflict-resolution skills.

Q. If mental self-defense skills can prevent students from fighting, isn't it enough to teach only those skills, rather than the physical ones?

A. It is the physical skills that give students self-confidence. Mental self-defense skills alone are not enough because of the fight-or-flight reaction. It's a matter of intelligently combining mental and physical skills into one comprehensive program that really works. Only with a complete set of skills are children prepared to cope with any conflict situation.

Q. Don't you think the world is getting to be less violent? I know we read so much in the papers about shootings and killings, but that's because the news focuses on these things, and because we are able to get much more news these days than we ever could before.

A. We all wish violence would go away. But we cannot avoid it by pretending it doesn't exist. The fact is that there is a terrible trend toward ever deadlier violence and a much younger age of those involved in it. I'm not trying to employ fear tactics, but we must accept that it exists, take it seriously, and get help. We cannot afford to wait until it is one of our children killed in our local school. That is reactive thinking. We need to proactively support this type education, which has the potential to create a safe and peaceful world for them, for us, and for all the generations to come.

Q. You've stayed with the martial arts all these years and are a sixth-degree black belt now. What keeps you going?

A. What keeps me going is that I can see the incredible potential of the martial arts especially as it pertains to our children. I have five daughters. We need to help our children learn to stop this terrible violence they live with each day.

Q. What do you see as the most important aspects of the martial arts, especially with relation to young people?

A. I see the martial arts as a possible way for young people to understand and resolve conflict before it begins. They can be trained to do so. And I think this training has global ramifications. If we learn early on how to resolve conflict peacefully, it is going to affect how we act as adults—at home, at work, and in the world.

Q. What do you think is the most important martial art?

A. The main goal of all martial arts is to understand and resolve conflict peacefully. My particular martial art has been karate, mainly Japanese. I've also studied other martial arts throughout the years. But I think what I say pertains to all types or styles of martial arts.

Q. Are you saying that there is a common intent underlying all martial arts, a universal foundation to them?

A. Yes, and I think that has been generally overlooked. Some individual martial arts teachers have pointed this out, but mainly the martial arts have been taught at the physical level. I call this the tertiary, or third, level. At this level, we manage conflict by physical means. The emphasis has been on physical self-defense and tournaments, which have a place. But for the martial arts to grow and meet the needs of deeper individual and social concerns, it must go beyond the physical. Answers to our urgent problems of violence in our relationships with other people must go beyond self-defense skills.

Q. What are the deeper insights contained in the martial arts that can address all the violence in our society? Aren't we asking too much of the martial arts to solve this tremendous problem?

A. Let me create a picture for you. It's like building a house. You need to have a proper foundation. In karate you start with creating strong stances to give the students the proper foundation for their techniques. The same is true in creating a foundation for understanding and resolving conflict without using physical means. This foundation is what I call the primary, or first, level. At this level we understand the conflict facing us and our intention, at all costs, is to avoid the conflict, prevent it. This level can also be called the spiritual level, because it requires that we go into a deeper place within ourselves for answers.

Q. Are you advocating that we teach young people Asian philosophy or religion?

A. No. "Spiritual" is a word I use in a very qualified way since it has so many connotations. I am not advocating any established religious belief system or any Asian religion or philosophical way of thinking. All that I am saying is that, inherent in the martial arts themselves is a presence of mind that can understand conflict at its deepest level and end it there.

Q. Are you saying that there are levels or stages of development in the philosophical or nonphysical side of the martial arts?

A. I am also careful when using the word "philosophy," because it, too, has many meanings. Philosophy in this case does not mean my philosophy versus your philosophy. It means "the love of truth in everyday living." Unfortunately, what we have today are conflicting points of view about everything, including philosophy. We have "my" martial art versus "your" martial art. In society, we have "my" nation, race, religion versus "your" nation, race, religion. So much fragmentation, division, separation—conflict!

Q. Still, most people would think teaching martial arts to stop such conflict sounds contradictory.

A. As I mentioned earlier, this was the original intent of martial arts practice. In fact, the ancient Chinese character used to write "martial," pronounced *wu,* or *bu* in Japanese, is composed of two parts: a drawing that means "sword" and a drawing that means "stop." The goal of martial training, even three thousand years ago in China, was to put an end to conflict.

Q. Thus we must ARM our children to prevent violence.

A. Yes, exactly. The levels, or stages, of development in "conflict education," as I call it, are:

- The primary or **A**voiding level, which is the spiritual level;
- The secondary or **R**esolving level, which is the mental level; and
- The tertiary or **M**anaging level, which is the physical level.

When taught properly, the martial arts should include all three levels.

Q. So the real intention of the martial arts is to stop conflict before it starts. But if it starts, to be able to resolve it mentally, as you say, before it gets to the physical stage. Is this correct?

A. Exactly. This was historically true. I'm not making this up. Originally the martial arts were taught as a whole endeavor. They changed when they came to the West into fighting skills only and than competitive sport. We left the essence or the foundation of the martial arts in Asia, perhaps because we did not understand the underlying philosophical basis or thought it was in opposition to our Western way of thinking. If there were any attempts at understanding the nonphysical aspects back in the early days of martial arts in the West, these were, for the most part, either intellectual lip service or memorizing and reciting some sort of martial arts creed.

Q. Years ago, there were only adults attending martial arts classes. Today, according to statistics, seventy to eighty percent of martial arts students are young people. What has happened and how are we going to meet the needs of these young martial artists?

A. That is an excellent question, because we need to equip our children with the right skills to understand and resolve conflict peacefully. So many martial arts schools are still of the mind set that all we need to teach them are the physical skills or the sports aspect of the martial arts. These schools are growing complacent, because they are making a great deal of money from teaching the martial arts in this way. But they are not meeting the real needs of society.

People are beginning to discover the greater potential of these arts and are expecting more from them, especially parents and teachers. They see that the martial arts can help solve the problems kids face everyday. If these schools don't change and meet the needs of parents and the community, they will go out of business. The martial art school of the next century will offer much more than physical skills; it will provide a complete martial arts education that addresses all levels of conflict education. I'm very excited about that.

Q. If martial arts training has worked since its arrival in the West, why change it now?

A. I don't believe it is still working, and I'm not sure it ever did. The main reason for change, however, is that the times demand it. Years ago, if you had a disagreement, perhaps you might get into a fight and someone would get a black eye or a bloody lip, and that would be the end of it. Today, there are knives and guns, and what was once a fist fight is now a war. Children are seriously injured and even killed. So how do physical skills help now? You can't block or karate chop a bullet. You need to be able to get out of a potential conflict by using your brain, by using nonphysical means.

Q. Do you think television and the movies are working against martial arts philosophy?

A. There is definitely a relationship between actual violence and increasing portrayal of violence. There are people who say, "I watched horror movies as a kid, and I turned out okay." Yes. Me, too. But there have been over a thousand studies done since 1956 on whether violence on TV affects children's behavior, and every study has conclusively proven that it does. But somehow many people ignore these facts and say that their freedom to choose, their rights are being taken away. They forget that with rights go responsibilities. We can't simply accept chaos because we all want a license to do whatever we want.

Q. So you believe in freedom, but to a point.

A. One of the most important things the martial arts teaches, especially to young people, is respect. That means that they have respect for themselves and others, that there is a generally accepted code of conduct that lays out intelligent guidelines for behavior. We are trying to teach our children values, some structure for them to live within. Years ago the structure was too rigid, and we rebelled. Then the pendulum swung too far the other way, and we had almost a complete lack of structure. We said, "Do you own thing." I think we need a sensible balance, providing our young students in the martial arts with an education that helps them create the confidence to understand and resolve conflict peacefully, to build character by respecting all other human beings, and to understand how to live in this world intelligently, lovingly. This is the real intention of the martial arts.

Q. It sounds like you're saying that the martial arts is an education, not just a self-defense or a sport. If this is so, how does it compare to young people's academic education?

A. The martial arts *is* an education. It addresses the number one concern of society, violence in our relationships. There is no other endeavor I know that can address conflict or violence on all levels—physically, mentally, and spiritually. I know this may seem a contradiction because the general public mainly sees the martial arts as just more violence—and they are right when it is taught only as a physical self-defense. But if taught properly, wholly, it has the most incredible potential of all human endeavors to resolve conflict peacefully.

Q. What place does the martial arts teacher play in this ?

A. The place of the martial arts teacher is to educate him or herself as a Martial Arts for Peace educator. This means going beyond the skill of being a martial arts coach or self-defense instructor. It means that he or she will have to be educated in the spiritual and mental aspects of the martial arts, the skills of understanding and resolving conflict nonviolently, before it gets to the physical level. This means thinking beyond the playground, beyond our communities. It means seeing the larger picture—

stopping violence in the world, and especially the most extreme violence, war.

Q. You believe the martial arts can do that?

A. The martial arts has the potential to do that. Martial Arts for Peace educators can help their students understand all aspects of conflict, so that when they grow into adulthood, they will have the intelligence and skill to create a new world, because they been properly educated to do so. Today, young people are mainly trained intellectually and vocationally, which is necessary, but this training does not address the larger issue of relationships. Training in relationship skills, and understanding the conditioning that prevents good relationships—these are the real basics of this education, and of the martial arts as well.

For further information about the Martial Arts Partners for Peace programs, contact the Atrium Society at 1-800-848-6021 or at www.atriumsoc.org.

ABOUT THE AUTHOR

Dr. Terrence Webster-Doyle holds a Ph.D. in Health and Human Services as well as a sixth-degree black belt in martial arts, and is co-founder and volunteer director of Martial Arts Partners for Peace and the Atrium Society, a non-profit organization. Dr. Webster Doyle is a parent and former school teacher and administrator who has taught at the secondary, community college, and university level, in psychology, education, and philosophy, and served as a juvenile delinquency prevention task force member.

Drawing on his diverse background of forty years experience in conflict education, Dr. Webster-Doyle developed his unique "How To Defeat the Bully Without Fighting Program" and has written seventeen books and eleven curricula in support of it. The program, which includes a book, curriculum, a workbook, two videos and poster, is actively in use in hundreds of schools in the U.S. and around the world. The program focuses on his best-selling book, *Why Is Everybody Always Picking On Me?: A Guide to Handling Bullies*, which has helped thousands of young people worldwide to cope with the problem of bullying.

Dr. Webster-Doyle's internationally acclaimed Martial Arts for Peace and Education for Peace books have earned him the Benjamin Franklin Award for Excellence in Independent Publishing for six consecutive years. His Martial Arts for Peace books and programs have been endorsed by the National PTA, *Scouting Magazine* (for the Boy Scouts and Girl Scouts of America), National Education Association (NEA), Educators for Social Responsibility and the International Association of Educators for World Peace (NGO, UNESCO, UNICEF), and others. He was also awarded the prestigious Robert Burns Medal in literature by Austria's Albert Schweitzer Society for "outstanding merit in the field of peace promotion." A three-time Martial Arts Hall of Fame inductee, he has been featured worldwide in the media, including a feature article in *Sports Illustrated for Kids*.

To order Dr. Webster-Doyle's books contact Weatherhill, Inc., at (tel) 800-437-7840, (fax) 800-557-5601, or (e-mail) weatherhill@weatherhill.com.

WHY IS EVERYBODY ALWAYS PICKING ON ME? A complete program for helping young people to peacefully avoid or resolve conflict, including stories, roleplaying, problem-solving, and other activities that teach both mental and physical self-defense skills. Includes a step-by-step program for dealing with bullies. Suitable for young people ages 8 through 18 and their parents.

8 1/2 X 9 1/2; 144 PP; 21 FULL-COLOR ILLUSTRATIONS; ISBN 0-8348-0467-0; $14.95 (PB)

Tales of the Empty-handed Masters

Classic Martial Arts Books for Young People by Dr. Terrence Webster-Doyle

Martial Arts for Peace books offer young people a view of the martial arts as they should be seen: as a healthy and humane activity that can help them to live with sensitivity and intelligence.

Eye of the Hurricane
Embarks on the journey into the heart of "Empty Self," the path of self-confidence and nonviolent inner power.
8 1/2 x 9 1/2; 128 pp; 20 color illustrations; ISBN 0-942941-24-1;
$14.95 (pb)

Maze of the Fire Dragon
Travels further with symbolic challenges that lead the reader to understand his or her real strengths.
8 1/2 x 9 1/2; 128 pp; 20 color illustrations; ISBN 0-942941-26-8;
$14.95 (pb)

Flight of the Golden Eagle
Offers insights for understanding conflict, guiding the martial artist to live with awareness and intelligence.
8 1/2 x 9 1/2; 112 pp; 20 color illustrations; ISBN 0-942941-28-4;
$14.95 (pb)

Breaking the Chains of the Ancient Warrior
Depicts the profound mental and physical training of martial arts students. Through classic martial arts stories and the author's own experience, this book teaches the most important lesson of all: Respect.
8 1/2 x 9 1/2; 172 pp; 22 color illustrations; ISBN 0-942941-32-2;
$14.95 (pb)

The "weathermark" identifies this book as a production of Weatherhill, Inc., publishers of fine books on Asia and the Pacific. Editorial supervision: Ray Furse. Book and cover design: Mariana Canelo. Production supervision: Bill Rose. Printing and binding: R. R. Donnelley. The typeface used is Minion.